THE CRYPTIDS OF ASIA AND OCEANIA

THE MYTHS AND HISTORICAL ROOTS OF UNDISCOVERED CREATURES

CAROL SCOTT

BEYOND THE FRAY

Publishing

ISBN 13: 978-1-954528-50-5

Cover design: Disgruntled Dystopian Publications

Beyond The Fray Publishing, a division of Beyond The Fray, LLC, San
Diego, CA
www.beyondthefraypublishing.com

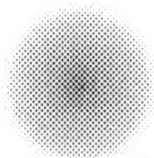

BEYOND THE FRAY

Publishing

CONTENTS

DEDICATION

To my parents, who always encouraged my fascination with cryptozoology,

&

Todd Gray, my middle school science teacher, who dared me to host a lesson on cryptids for my peers.

The most beautiful thing we can experience is the mysterious. It is the source of all true art and science. He to whom the emotion is a stranger, who can no longer pause to wonder and stand wrapped in awe, is as good as dead; his eyes are closed.

– Albert Einstein

INTRODUCTION

During the Dutch colonization of Indonesia, rumors abounded about a giant lizard, sometimes referred to as a crocodile or a dragon by whoever told of the creature, on the island of Komodo. In 1910, an adventurous military commander, Lieutenant van Steyn van Hensbroek, traveled from the nearby island of Flores to Komodo to investigate these reports. He returned with a photo and the skin of the animal, which he sent to Pieter Ouwens, then director of the Java Zoological Museum and Botanical Gardens in Buitenzorg, who identified the animal as a large monitor lizard. Realizing that the animal was new to science – in fact, it would upend scientific assumptions about reptile size – Ouwens published the first formal description of the animal, which we commonly know now as the Komodo dragon, *Varanus komodoensis*. News of this scientific marvel quickly spread, resulting in various expeditions to bring Komodo dragons, both alive and deceased, to other parts of the world, which allegedly inspired the seminal 1933 film *King Kong*, with Indonesia serving as Earth's final "Lost World."[1]

The Komodo dragon is hardly alone as an example of megafauna that long escaped Western scientific knowledge. In the twentieth century, other creatures that are now well-known, such as the okapi (1901), mountain gorilla (1902), giant panda (1916), colossal squid (1925), bonobo (1928), and Saola / Vu Quang ox (1992), were dismissed as scientifically implausible by Western scientists despite being known to locals in their habitat. Coelacanths, an order of large fish closely related to lungfish and tetrapods, are an even more remarkable story, as the entire genus was believed extinct for sixty-six million years until one was caught off the coast of South Africa in 1938, followed by another species in Indonesia in 1998. Of note, locals in Indonesia did not think much of the coelacanth; researchers were initially made aware of the species after seeing one for sale in a market the year prior.

These miraculous discoveries serve as a reminder of the hidden biodiversity of our world and serve as a warning against assuming that non-Western beliefs hold no potential for scientific thought.

Today, the search for undiscovered animals continues. Cryptozoology, which translates from Greek as "the study of hidden animals," is a field that aims to prove the existence of animals that are not widely accepted by the scientific community. These animals range from those said to be extinct to creatures lacking conclusive proof of their existence, or even just animals well outside their natural range.

Cryptozoologists rely primarily on witness testimony and on miscellaneous pieces of evidence such as footprints, hair, and sounds that cannot be traced to any known animal.

While the number of cryptids, those animals not accepted by science, is innumerable, several have taken hold in the popular consciousness, such as the North American Bigfoot, the yeti of the Himalayas, the chupacabra, and the Loch Ness Monster of Scotland. These four are among the most fantastical and also the most searched-for cryptids, resulting in much more media coverage and presentation than other cryptids.

While many cryptids are overlooked in favor of those four creatures, Asia and Oceania have a plethora of rarely discussed creatures. Some, like the Tasmanian tiger or moa, are creatures that have become extinct in modern times due to the actions of humans, while the ancient giant shark megalodon reputedly went extinct millions of years ago. "Living dinosaurs" also have their place in the cryptozoology of the area, with creatures such as the ahool, ropen, and row being interpreted as dinosaurs that survived the Cretaceous-Paleogene (K-Pg) extinction event. Australian mythology contains a bountiful number of references to creatures, such as the bunyip, that have continued their legacy into the realm of cryptozoology. Australia, New Zealand, and the various southeast islands even have their own reports of Sasquatch-type creatures. While some of the creatures in this book are more reasonable than others, one might still question the ability of a creature to hide in our modern era. However, even large animals (referred to as megafauna) have been discovered around the world after being dismissed. In the late '90s and into the 2000s, the discovery of animals, such as Vietnam's saola or the Sundaland clouded leopard of Malaysia proved that there are still mammals waiting to be discovered. Those suggesting that creatures should have been found by now must take into account the small number of works that document the areas many of these cryptids are said to live in, which consist of treacherous areas such as dense jungles and the Outback. Only continued investigations into the Earth that we live on will reveal what these remote areas contain.

One particular note about investigations and this book: I have done my best to include non-Western sources, from the early reports to more recent work done by scientists and investigators from the areas written about in this book. As demonstrated with the "discovery" of the Komodo dragon and the Coelacanth, Western researchers often ignore the residents of these regions, to science's detriment. There are, quite admittedly, gaps in this book – for various reasons, texts and oral histories of these creatures were not recorded or were lost. Sometimes offhand mentions by Western explorers form the backbone of our knowledge about cryptids. This was even noted by renowned crypto-zoologist Ivan T. Sanderson in 1961 in his seminal *Abominable Snowmen*. One can imagine the continued issue of these texts not being prioritized for archivable purposes for reasons including racism and a disregard for indigenous storytelling.

A focus of further investigations should be the preservation of historical facts. While there's certainly value in exploring the reported locations of cryptids, investigating historical accounts and making sure that history is preserved is vital. Those who are able to travel to the locations in this book would be wise to consider investigating local libraries and archives for information that has not been translated or made its way to the public. Consider speaking with scientists, folklorists, and other researchers from the local area. One of the most rewarding experiences in this book was speaking with an expert on the Nittaewo of Sri Lanka, which is covered later in this book. Speaking with locals in the area can reveal new areas of inquiries and provide context that one may not necessarily consider as an outsider.

Additionally, the cryptozoology community simply needs to do better in regard to scientific inquiry. To quote skeptic and anthropologist David J. Daegling in his *Bigfoot Exposed: An Anthropologist Examines America's Enduring Legend*:

> It is a fair point echoed across the board by the advocates; the scientific establishment seems to reject Bigfoot reflexively without so much as feigning an interest in examining the evidence.
>
> It is worth a digression on what exactly we mean when we agree to analyze something "scientifically." In

one sense, science is little more than a protocol for observation and explanation. What distinguishes a scientific explanation from a nonscientific one is a willingness to test (either by further observation, experimentation, or prediction) whether or not a proposed explanation is reasonable and sufficient to account for an observation, however mundane or bizarre. In this sense, there is nothing mysterious about practicing science; it involves looking at and manipulating the world in a systematic way so that we can make generalizations about how things work. It is the basis for reliable knowledge, as opposed to anecdotal knowledge. The distinction is important.

The anecdote is the single observation or a collection of stories that, after the fact, do not permit confirmation for any number of reasons. An anecdote isn't necessarily false, it is just unverifiable. Seeing a hairy monster while driving alone at night is a tailor-made anecdote; even if you remember the time and the exact spot on the highway and return with your friends to the scene to find giant footprints, the hairy giant part of your story is still anecdote. The footprints are the facts of the matter. These can be treated scientifically for a couple of reasons: first, you can measure and record them, and second, other people can look at the imprints as well.[2]

To put my frustration simply: I do not disagree with the

search for undiscovered animals. I believe there are creatures out there that are currently not recognized by science, and I'm not just referring to tiny bugs or amphibians. However, I have long been disappointed by the community at large retreating from basic scientific principles. That is not to say that everyone in the community does so – Jeff Meldrum and Karl Shuker are among those in the cryptozoology field who analyze evidence through a scientific lens. While the two researchers I listed are scientists (both have PhDs in scientific disciplines), I do not think that higher-quality research is limited to those who have studied in disciplines such as zoology or anthropology. The scientific method is a great model, but rarely followed. The study of cryptozoology would benefit from engaging in more rigorous investigations – from the work of Meldrum and Shuker in published works and journals to efforts such as the Encounter Reports Database and Sightings Map that the North American Wood Ape Conservancy maintains, which allows for more cross-referencing of reported sightings.[3] The tools are available; they must be used.

I have formatted this book as more of a reference text. One can read a select entry without having to read previous entries. Chapters focus on the historical accounts of the cryptid, with many chapters including a linguistic breakdown of the name of the creature if appropriate. Many chapters end with theories presented by cryptozoologists, scientists, and other researchers. I make no claim to presenting a definitive reasoning for any of the cryptids, but I do hope that this book leads to further investigations on these creatures.

In the words of Bernard Heuvelmans in his seminal work *On the Track of Unknown Animals*, "I can only leave the reader to draw his own conclusions."[4]

CHAPTER 1

AUSTRALIA

Bunyip

STORIES OF THE BUNYIP, generally translated as "devil" or "evil spirit," began with the Indigenous populations of Australia.[1] According to the Dreamtime legends, the bunyip is a river spirit that will eat anything too close to the river shore, including livestock and children. The lore regarding the creation of this beast states that a man named Bunyip broke the great law of the Rainbow Serpent by eating his totem animal. The good spirit Biami cursed Bunyip into an evil spirit who lured its victims to it.

An early account from 1847 describes the creature as such:

> ...much dreaded by them [the locals]...It inhabits the Murray; but...they have some difficulty describing it. Its most usual form...is said to be that of an enormous starfish.[2]

Common features in many nineteenth-century news-paper accounts include a doglike face, a crocodile-like head, dark fur, a horselike tail, flippers, and walrus-like tusks or horns or a duck-like bill, indicating that early colonialists may have been influenced by strange discoveries of the era such as the duck-billed platypus and "half-zebra, half-giraffe" quagga. More modest accounts tell of a creature about four to five feet in length with the body of a calf or seal and a head resembling that of a dog, as well as possessing long fangs and sharp claws.[3] However, reports are not consistent across Australia, indicating possible misidentifications or even cultural memories.

Some believe that reports of the bunyip are sightings of a living population of *Diprotodon australis*, the largest marsupial that ever existed. An example of the Australian megafauna of the Pleistocene epoch, the *Diprotodon* is believed to have gone extinct about forty-six thousand years ago. The more conventional explanation is that the original tales of the bunyip are about the last remnants of the *Diprotodon*, which would have been alive at the time of the expected arrival of humans in Australia. Further reports are, according to this theory, a result of the cultural memory of the *Diprotodon*.[4] Paleontologist Pat Vickers-Rich and geologist Neil Archbold also suggested that Indigenous legends "perhaps had stemmed from an acquaintance with prehistoric bones or even living prehistoric animals themselves...When confronted with the remains of some of the now-extinct Australian marsupials, Aborigines would often identify them as the bunyip."[5]

Another explanation for the sightings in the nineteenth century were reports of seals that would swim up the Murray and Darling Rivers. Postulated by Charles Fenner in 1933, Fenner notes accounts of elephant seals and leopard seals that have made the journey upriver.[6] Such animals would have been strange even to the natives of the area.

Burrunjor

From the wilds of the Outback come reports of a living *Tyrannosaurus rex*. An object of interest for Young Earth Creationists, the creature has also been studied in depth by Australian cryptozoologist Rex Gilroy, notably in his publication *Burrunjor! The Search For Australia's Living Tyrannosaurus*. Gilroy recounts one supposed encounter with this creature:

In 1978, a Northern Territory bushman and explorer, Bryan Clark, related a story of his own that had taken place some years before. While mustering cattle in the Urupunji area, he became lost in the remote wilderness of that part of Arnhem Land. It took him three days to find his way out of that region and back to the homestead from which he had originally set out. He didn't know it at the time, but his footprints had been picked up and followed by two Aboriginal trackers and a mounted policeman. On the first night of their search they camped on the outskirts of the Burrunjor scrub, even though the two trackers protested strongly in doing so. The policeman hobbled his horse, cooked their meal and then climbed into his swag and went to sleep. Later that night the two Aborigines, shouting unintelligibly and grasping for their packs and saddles, suddenly woke him up. The policeman realized at this moment the ground appeared to be shaking. Hurriedly getting to his feet, he, too, gathered up his belongings. Shortly afterwards the three galloped away. The policeman told Bryan Clark later at the Urapunji homestead that he also heard a sound, somewhat like a loud puffing or grunting noise, certainly loud enough to be coming from a large animal. When asked if he intended to include this in his report, the policeman replied that he would not because he feared that no one would believe him. The policeman warned Bryan Clark never to return to that area, because if he got lost there again, he would be "on his own": the police would not come looking for him.[7]

Legends of a large bipedal creature also appear in the Dreamtime legend. Gilroy has collected pictograph artwork that seem to show the popular depiction of a *T. rex*, although these have yet to be verified as authentic.[8] Although the consensus in the realm of cryptozoology is that the creature is a living *T. rex*, reports of the creature also resemble types of archosaurs such as the effigia, a fossil known only from New Mexico. With few verifiable sources and even less evidence, it's unlikely that this living dinosaur continues to exist to this day.

Megalania

Perhaps one of the most fearsome reptiles to ever exist, the *Megalania* was part of the megafauna that developed over the centuries on the Australian continent.[9] The reptile is estimated to have been somewhere from 5.5 to 7.9 meters long, thus classifying it as the largest terrestrial lizard known to have existed.[10] Feeding upon medium to large marsupials, the lizard was possibly able to run around three kilometers per hour.[11] Some researchers have even suggested that, like its living cousin the Komodo dragon, it could spew venom.[12] The creature overall has been described as a giant Komodo dragon.[13]

Supposedly driven to extinction around fifty-thousand years ago by other predators or the arrival of humans and their ability to utilize fire, some have suggested a later date of extinction for the *Megalania*, based on the Bundjalung Nation Dreamtime legend Dirawong, a god described as similar to a *Megalania* that gives the nation the tools and knowledge to survive.[14] Based on the time of arrival of the Indigenous population of Australia, this could indicate a time of extinction for the *Megalania* around the end of the last ice age, twelve thousand years ago.

While the Outback is still a treacherous place to explore, it is unlikely that such a large and ferocious predator could evade any sightings over several thousand years, making it an unlikely case for still being extant.

Megalodon

Regarded as one of the fiercest creatures to ever exist, the megalodon, a relative of the great white shark, is estimated to have been 10.5 meters long on average, with a potential maximum length of 18 meters. The species fed on large prey, such as whales, seals, and sea turtles, while inhabiting warm coastal waters around the world. Fossils, predominately teeth, have been found near Australia, New Zealand, Fiji, and French Polynesia. The creature, by all scientific estimates, went extinct 3.6 million years ago. Distribution patterns show that various prey of the megalodon experienced a boon from its extinction, with the great white shark extending into its former habitat.[15] Supposedly fresh teeth, such as those erroneously dated as being only eleven thousand years old from the HMS *Challenger*, have been found to have a lower rate of decomposition that made early dating produce poor results.[16]

While sightings have occurred sporadically prior to 2013, belief in the continued existence of the megalodon gained more widespread acceptance after Animal Planet ran the mockumentary *Megalodon: The Monster Shark Lives*, which presented itself as a documentary on scientific evidence that the shark could still be alive. However, the documentary itself is entirely fictional, with the "scientists" interviewed being paid actors. The mockumentary drew the ire of many in the scientific community for airing without disclaimers.[17]

As the ReefQuest Centre for Shark Research writes on the idea that megalodon has survived in the deep sea:

> Although very little abyssal life has been sampled, the deep-sea is a very difficult environment demanding numerous significant specializations. Amount of food in the deep-sea is not the issue. Megalodon seems to have been limited to warm, shallow seas near coastlines and there is no evidence it had any specializations that would have enabled it to survive the intense cold of the deep-sea.[18]

While the continued existence of the megalodon is unlikely, we (and our love of swimming) are probably better off for it.

Queensland Tiger

As the name might suggest, the Queensland "tiger" is a striped cryptid reported to roam the wilds of the Australian province of Queensland. The creature was described as a "striped marsupial cat" in Australian zoologist A. S. le Souef's *The Wild Animals of Australasia*.[19] Bernard Heuvelmans noted that the creature, featured in several early twentieth-century books on Australian zoology, such as le Souef's work, had arguably become one of the cryptids most likely to be discovered.

Reports of a strange creature in the wilderness areas of northeast Queensland begin with the local Indigenous population, who referred to the creature as the yarri.[20] Norwegian zoologist Carl Lumholtz, who spent time with the native populations in 1880–84, records stories of the *yarri* in his seminal *Among Cannibals* (1889):

> It was said to be about the size of a dingo, though its legs were shorter and tail long, and it was described by the blacks as being very savage. If pursued it climbed up the trees, where the natives did not dare follow it, and by gestures they explained to me how at such times it would growl and bite their hands. Rocky retreats were its most favourite habitat, and its principal food was said to be a little brown variety of wallaby common in north Queensland scrubs.[21]

Lumholtz's work did lead to the recognition of one animal, albeit not the Queensland tiger. Instead, the boongary, a then-unknown species of tree kangaroo, was recognized and christened *Dendrolagus lumholtzi* in his honour.[22]

So why has the yarri not received the same recognition? More reports came in the early twentieth century as Queensland became more colonized, with notable sightings by the police magistrate, Brinsley G. Sheridan, and Robert Johnstone of the native police.[23] With numerous sightings, the yarri was nearly accepted as fact, as can be seen with le Souef's article on the creature in his work.

Several carcasses have also been reported: J. McGeehan supposedly found a yarri that his dogs had killed around 1900; a man named Woods reported that a farmhand felled a creature in the late 1920s; two corpses were mentioned in le Souef's work. However, the Woods specimen was devoured by dogs and the other carcasses were apparently discarded; thus, their authenticity was not verified by science.[24]

While reports, and perhaps carcasses, were plentiful in the early twentieth century, these have dropped off since the mid-1950s. In the book *Out of the Shadows*, researchers Tony Healy and Paul Cropper speculate that the yarri may be extinct, a victim of dingo traps and the lethally poisonous cane toad, an invasive species present in Australia since the 1930s.[25] Rex Gilroy, a well-known Australian cryptozoologist, continues to collect sparse accounts of the Queensland tiger.[26]

So just what is (or was) the Queensland tiger? Skeptics identify it as an oversized domestic cat, misidentified dog or dingo, or, surprisingly enough, an escaped tiger. Dr. Karl Shuker regards these as "woefully ill-founded," saying:

> Characteristics such as its distinctive hoop-like stripes, protruding tusk-like teeth, tree-climbing prowess, and longstanding aboriginal knowledge of its existence (to the extent that it has its own name) at once discount all of those identities and label it as a bonafide native species...[27]

Two common identities are suggested for the Queensland tiger. One is the Tasmanian tiger, better known as the thylacine. Denounced as extinct from the mainland for 2,300 or so years, the thylacine was found on the nearby island of Tasmania until the supposed last one died in captivity in 1936.[28] While the continued existence of the thylacine in Tasmania is discussed in the next chapter, some have suggested that the yarri is – or was – a mainland variant of the thylacine. This theory was proposed in the 1965 revision of Ellis Troughton's book *Furred Animals of Australia*.[29] (38) However, Dr. Karl Shuker notes some logical leaps in describing the Queensland tiger as the thylacine: "...a dog-headed creature with stripes only upon the upper portion of its back is hardly a plausible identity for an effortlessly arboreal, cat-headed beast with hoop-like bands sometimes encircling its entire body."[30]

Perhaps more intriguing is the thought that the yarri could be related to, or even a surviving population of, the *Thylacoleo carnifex*, the marsupial lion of Australia. Reconstructions of fossilized remains depict a cat-shaped animal the size of a leopard with a powerful jaw, long limbs, a pseudo-opposable thumb on each forepaw, and huge tusk-like teeth projecting outwards. Such a description is consistent with many reports of the yarri, in particular many reports that focused on the distinctive "tusks" of the creature. However, *Thylacoleo* went extinct some sixteen thousand years ago. Dr. Shuker has suggested the possibility that the yarri is perhaps a modern-day descendant of *Thylacoleo* – given its tendency to be reported as smaller, this could be a possible fit for the strange creature.[31]

From once being an almost accepted fact to becoming a notorious cryptid, the Queensland tiger is a mysterious beast in Australian cryptozoology. One hopes that, if a population still survives, it could become one of the twenty-first century's greatest zoological (re)discoveries.

Thylacine

The thylacine, suffering from government-sponsored hunting and habitat loss, is believed to have gone extinct when Benjamin, a captive male at the Hobart Zoo in Tasmania, died as a result of neglect in 1936. The thylacine, also known as the Tasmanian tiger due to its stripes, was declared extinct in 1982 after it had not been conclusively spotted in the wild for fifty years.[32] Several searches were carried out up to the 1960s with minor successes, with the 1959–1961 expeditions led by Dr. Eric Guiler finding evidence of tracks, vocalizations, and anecdotal evidence.[33] The three Guiler expeditions remain the best evidence that the thylacine survived to at least the 1960s. Further expeditions in the 1970s, led by zoologist Jeremy Griffith and later the Thylacine Expeditionary Research Team with environmentalist Dr. Bob Brown, yielded no evidence.[34] Researcher Michael Moss used the Australian Freedom of Information Act to access government records of the thylacine, with the Tasmanian Parks and Wildlife Service concluding:

> Since 1936, no conclusive evidence of a thylacine has been found. However, the incidence of reported thylacine sightings has continued. Most sightings occur at night, in the north of the State, in or near areas where suitable habitat is still available. Although the species is now considered to be "probably extinct," these sightings provide some hope that the thylacine may still exist.[35]

Overall, there are more than a dozen reports collected between 1996 and 2001.[36]

In 2005, Klaus Emmerichs, a German tourist, captured an alleged photograph of a thylacine near the Lake St Clair National Park, but the photos were found to be inconclusive, and their authenticity was never established. The most likely record of the species' persistence was proposed by Athol Douglas in the journal *Cryptozoology*, where Douglas challenges the carbon dating of the specimen found at Mundrabilla in South Australia as 4,500 years old; Douglas proposed instead that the well-preserved thylacine carcass was several months old when discovered. Despite Douglas' argument, the specimen has not been reassessed as of 2022.

The Department of Primary Industries, Parks, Water and Environment released a document compiling eight sightings between September 1, 2016, and September 16,

2019, indicating that the Tasmanian and Australian governments still hold interest in recovering evidence of the species.[37] Despite numerous multimillion-dollar rewards being offered for conclusive evidence or a captured thylacine, the species is regarded as extinct without evidence being presented without a doubt. Sightings will likely continue and hopefully be recorded by researchers and officials, creating a resource for scientists to study if the species is found.

Yowie

One of the most enduring stories of the Indigenous people of Australia is that of the yowie. A version of the Sasquatch from the Land Down Under, the tales of the Indigenous people speak of their ancestors arriving in Australia and encountering an aggressive species of ape-men. The new arrivals to the continent defeated the ape-men due to their superior weapons.

The description of the yowie is presented in this 1842 piece from the *Australian and New Zealand Monthly Magazine*:

> The natives of Australia...believe in...[the] Yahoo...This being they describe as resembling a man...of nearly the same height...with long white hair hanging down from the head over the features...the arms as extraordinarily long, furnished at the extremities with great talons, and the feet turned backwards, so that, on flying from man,

the imprint of the foot appears as if the being had trav-
elled in the opposite direction. Altogether, they
describe it as a hideous monster of an unearthly character and ape-like appearance.[38]

Some Indigenous accounts suggest that the creature is
a part of the Dreamtime mythology:

> Old Bungaree, a Gunedah aboriginal...said at one time
> there were tribes of them [yahoos] and they were the
> original inhabitants of the country – he said they were
> the old race of blacks... [the yahoos] and the blacks used
> to fight and the blacks always beat them, but the yahoo
> always made away – being faster runners.[39]

Modern accounts of the yowie generally describe the
creature as being 2.1 to 3.6 meters tall (between 6 feet, 11
inches and 12 feet) with large footprints and a broad, flat
nose.[40] Reports vary on its temperament, with some
reporting aggression similar to the original Indigenous
legend, including a case in which a yowie reportedly
brutalized a dog.[41] However, other reports characterize it
as docile. Many modern reports occur in and around the
Blue Mountains area that is commonly termed the Sydney
Basin.[42]

Tony Healy and Paul Cropper collected over three
hundred reports of the yowie in their seminal work *The
Yowie: In Search of Australia's Bigfoot*, one of the greatest
works on the creature, covering reports from the historical

period to the modern age. The authors note a stunning lack of evidence for the creature – unlike its American counterpart, there are no recorded vocalizations, footage à la the famous Patterson-Gimlin film, or even footprints of a notably great quality.[43] Such makes the study of the yowie invariably difficult, with little to go on beyond quick sightings.

Few sources have suggested that the yowie is anything other than an ape creature in the vein of Sasquatch or the yeti. Most skeptics offer a combination of hoaxes, cultural mythology, and misidentification as explanations for sightings of the creature, which provides for the lack of presentable evidence despite its long history and a preponderance of sightings.[44]

Blue Mountains Panther

Phantom cats or alien big cats aren't supernatural, but rather creatures that are reported outside of their normal range with no immediately discernible explanation. One famous example of these ABCs is the Blue Mountains panther, a phantom cat reported in the Blue Mountains region just west of Sydney, New South Wales, for over a century.

Researchers on the topic have linked reports of the Blue Mountains panther to military mascots during World War II, escapee circus cats, and cats bought on the black market that have been released by the "owners."[45]

Over five hundred sightings have been recorded over

the past century, and several animals have been found mauled. The most recent animal to fall victim to the alleged predator was a pet alpaca in 2011; an autopsy revealed seven-centimeter puncture wounds to the skull. A report by the Hawkesbury area ranger concluded it may have been killed by a large cat.[46]

Humans have also allegedly been attacked by the Blue Mountains panther; notably, in 2002, a Kenthurst teenager named Luke Walker was attacked by what he stated to be a large feline; he suffered deep lacerations.[47]

Reports have continued up to 2020, where the panther was reported around the grounds of Sydney Adventist Hospital, Wahroonga.[48] The Instagram collective @bluemtns_explore posted pictures of alleged big cat tracks in April 2021.[49]

The NSW Department of Primary Industries (NPWS) has commissioned four reports into the phenomenon, in 1999, 2003, 2008/9 and 2013.[50] The 1999 report concluded that there was likely a small population of big cats in the area.[51] The initial research request was made of wildlife ecologist Johannes Bauer of the then-NSW Agriculture in 1999. His one-page report returned the following conclusion: "Difficult as it seems to accept, the most likely explanation of the evidence...is the presence of a large feline predator."[52]

The 2008 report, which was not released to the public, concluded:

There is no scientific evidence found during this review that conclusively proves the presence of free ranging exotic large cats in NSW, but a presence cannot be discounted, and it seems more likely than not on available evidence that such animals do exist in NSW.

However, the 2009 report offered:

Whilst information has been provided, there is still nothing to conclusively say that a large black cat exists.[53]

Residents have complained of a government cover-up, with the reasoning for the alleged cover-up differing by each person.

As of 2022, all evidence has been "soft" evidence (eyewitness reports, footprints, etc.), with researched "hard" evidence (scat, hair, etc.) being found to belong to other animals. The NSW Department of Primary Industries (DPI) maintains that reports of panthers in the area are actually feral cats, or even mistaken residents seeing wallabies in the dark.[54]

CHAPTER 2

CHINA

Yeren

AS WITH THE YOWIE, the *yeren* (Chinese: 野人, "wild man") is the Chinese equivalent of the North American Bigfoot. Reports of hairy ape-men go back to ancient times (more specifically, the Warring States period, which lasted from approximately 475 BC to 221 BC). In Qu Yuan's *Jiu Ge* ("Nine Songs"), the ninth song speaks of a "mountain spirit" (Chinese: 山鬼; "shān guǐ"), which has been variously interpreted as a humanlike creature clad in a fig leaf, a demon, or an ogre. The *Erya*, which has been described as the oldest surviving Chinese "dictionary," mentions a creature using a character translated as "orangutan" (Chinese: 猩々; "xīngxing"), an animal not native to China. It could also be more generally translated to "ape."[1]

The term *yeren* originates from the Shennongjia (northwestern Hubei) area, where it has been reported since the sixteenth century. *Fangxianzhi*, the local journal, first mentioned the yeren in 1555. During the Qing dynasty (1644–1912), *Fangxianzhi* published an article that said a group of yeren inhabited caves in the mountains of Fangxian (about ninety kilometers north of Shennongjia) and ate domestic chickens and dogs.[2]

Scientific interest in the yeren began in the 1950s under the reign of Mao Zedong, tied to an increase in reports and similar interest in the yeti from Tibet. Prominent anthropologist Pei Wenzhong brought attention to these reports to Chinese and Soviet scientists. Other scientists interested in the yeren reports included Mao Guangnian and Wu Rukang. However, the Mao government attempted to suppress discussion of the yeren (as well as other pieces of folklore, including ghosts) due to the belief that superstitions would impact productivity. Various scientists continued to study the yeren, arguing that replacing folklore with scientific evidence would be beneficial. Mao Guangnian compared the link between yeren and folklore to how manatees inspired mermaid stories.[3] Towards the end of the Mao era, in 1974, historian Li Jian, the vice secretary of the Prefectural Propaganda Department of Shennongjia, recorded testimonies from locals regarding the yeren, the oldest occurring in 1945. This earned Li the nickname "the Minister of Yeren" from community members.[4] With restrictions lifted, Western works on the yeti and Sasquatch were translated into Chinese, resulting in an interest in ape-man creatures and a subsequent "yeren *fever*."

An expedition was launched in 1977 by the Chinese

Academy of Sciences and Professor Zhou Guoxing, along with 109 military personnel, zoologists, biologists, and photographers, to attempt to find a yeren in Shennongjia.[5] The size of this search party was subsequently decreed a nuisance to the attempt to find a yeren.[6] Additional expeditions were launched with smaller cohorts, although they were still unsuccessful in finding definitive proof of the yeren. Interestingly, these expeditions were quite successful in bridging the gap between government scientists and locals who believed in folklore.[7]

The lack of success in finding proof – hair samples and other cited evidence were found to belong to well-known local animals – decreased interest in the creature by the 1980s.[8] Some Chinese scientists continue to search for the creature, with Wild Man Research Association being founded in November 2009.[9] Vice president of the association, Wang Shancai of the Hubei Relics and Archaeology Institute, claims to have collected four hundred reports of the creature in the Shennongjia area over the last century.[10] However, reports have been much less frequent since the heyday of "yeren fever."

Explanations for the yeren are similar to those used to explain the North American Sasquatch. Mainstream scientists point to misidentification of local wildlife (for example, upright Asian black bears could be mistaken for a humanoid).[11] A prominent theory suggested by Chinese scientists during yeren fever and commonly suggested by modern cryptozoologists is that the yeren is a relict population or close relative of the *Gigantopithecus*, an extinct genus of ape from the Early to Middle Pleistocene of southern China.[12] Some locals compared their yeren sightings to ethnic minorities; one local stated that he "thought it was a local Wa woman climbing the mountains to collect pig food."[13]

With some Chinese academics continuing to investigate the yeren, perhaps we might one day have the answer to the question of what roams the Shennonjia area.

Lake Tianchi Monster

The Lake Tianchi Monster is China's very own lake monster, equivalent to Western examples such as the Loch Ness Monster and the Ogopogo. Lake Tianchi, also known as Heaven Lake or *Cheonji* Lake in Korean, is a volcanic lake located partly in Ryanggang Province, North Korea, and partly in Jilin Province, northeastern China, and is recognized as the deepest volcanic lake in China.[14]

Reports of the creature vary wildly in description. The first reported sighting occured in 1903, when a creature "resembling a huge buffalo with a deafening roar" attacked three people before being shot and returning to the waters of the lake.[15]

By 1986, over five hundred people had seen the creature, but reports varied. Some describe it with a doglike head, a seal-like head, or even a humanlike head with large eyes.[16] Some of these reports included seeing multiple creatures interacting with each other.[17]

In 2002, a local tourism official named Xue Junlin

reported to *The China Daily* that during the latest appearance, the creature came within ten meters of the shore and jumped out of the water "like a seal." Xue said the creature stayed visible for about ten minutes before returning to the water.[18]

In 2003, local government agents spotted up to twenty of the creatures in the lake. *The Beijing Youth Daily* spoke to provincial forestry bureau vice director Zhang Lufeng, who stated, "Within about 50 minutes, the monsters appeared five times...At times there was one, at times there were several. The last time, there were as many as about 20." He added that the creatures, two to three kilometers in the distance, appeared only as white or black spots, but from the ripples in the water, he and others determined the spots were "living beings."[19]

In 2005, a tourist named Zheng Changchun took a video of an alleged sighting of the creature that was allegedly viewed by the tourist's family and various others in the area.[20] However, the video appears to be lost or otherwise not available outside of China. Two years later, TV reporter Zhuo Yongsheng shot a video of three pairs of the alleged creatures. The footage was sent to Xinhua's Jilin provincial bureau and does not appear to be publicly available.[21]

While reported sightings appear to have slowed down, reports still reach Western news media occasionally. In 2019, the UK magazine *Express* reported on an alleged photo of a creature described as "a mysterious black object floating on the surface of the Tianchi Lake."[22]

While some have suggested that the monster is a remnant population of *plesiosaurs*, scientists have pointed out that the lake only dates back to AD 946, millions of years after the genus went extinct. Additionally, various Chinese scientists have expressed skepticism that any large creature would be able to survive in the lake given its recent history of volcanic activity and low level of food sources.[23]

Maltese Tiger

The Maltese tiger is a reported variant of the South Chinese tiger, a population of the big cat native to the southern China regions of the Fujian, Guangdong, Hunan and Jiangxi provinces. The Maltese variant was spotted various times in the twentieth century, primarily in the Fujian province. Interesting early reports come from American missionary Harry R. Caldwell and American explorer Roy Chapman Andrews. Andrews dedicates an entire chapter to the "blue tiger" in his 1918 book *Camps and Trails in China*, while Caldwell wrote about his experiences hunting the creature in the aptly named *Blue Tiger* (1924).[24] Andrews quotes Caldwell as such:

> I selected a spot upon a hilltop and cleared away the grass and ferns with a jack-knife for a place to tie the goat. I concealed myself in the bushes ten feet away to await the attack, but the unexpected happened and the tiger approached from the rear.

When I first saw the beast he was moving stealthily along a little trail just across a shallow ravine. I supposed, of course, that he was trying to locate the goat which was bleating loudly, but to my horror I saw that he was creeping upon two boys who had entered the ravine to cut grass. The huge brute moved along lizard-fashion for a few yards and then cautiously lifted his head above the grass. He was within easy springing distance when I raised my rifle, but instantly I realized that if I wounded the animal the boys would certainly meet a horrible death.

Tigers are usually afraid of the human voice so instead of firing I stepped from the bushes, yelling and waving my arms. The huge cat, crouched for a spring, drew back, wavered uncertainly for a moment, and then slowly slipped away into the grass. The boys were saved but I had lost the opportunity I had sought for over a year.

However, I had again seen the animal about which so many strange tales had been told. The markings of the beast are strikingly beautiful. The ground color is of a delicate shade of maltese, changing into light gray-blue on the underparts. The stripes are well defined and like those of the ordinary yellow tiger.[25]

Of the main line of the South Chinese tiger, it is likely to be extinct in the wild, although it is currently listed as Critically Endangered on the IUCN Red List.[26] As such, the Maltese colour variant may never be seen again.

It is worth noting that a report of a blue tiger from Dr. Karl Shuker's *Mystery Cats of the World* comes from the Korean Demilitarized Zone.[27] This may be a variant of the Siberian tiger, which once roamed the Korean peninsula, although the current range of the Siberian tiger is only the Russian Far East.[28] Although no blue tigers have ever been captured or pelts recovered, a blue tiger was allegedly born at the Oklahoma Zoo in 1964, although it died in infancy and was not preserved or photographed.[29]

CHAPTER 3

INDIA

Monkey-man of Delhi

THE MONKEY-MAN OF NEW DELHI, as this interesting creature was known, terrorized the capital city of India for several weeks in 2001, with a few sporadic reports in 2002. Reports peaked from May 10 to about May 25 of the former year.

A contemporary report published in *The Guardian* describes the creature as such:

> The monkey-man, who is between four and five feet tall, has a "monkey like face," and strikes between midnight and 4am, has pounced on almost 20 victims during the past five days, leaving them with deep scratch marks and gouges on their arms and necks... Some victims say he wears a helmet; others insist that he sports metal claws, has a shaggy black hide – and possibly roller-skates.[1]

During the two weeks of the primary occurrence of reports, some four hundred people made calls to the police for allegedly being attacked by the bizarre creature. A study on alleged victims published in the *Indian Journal of Medical Sciences* identified the typical profile of a victim: "Majority of victims were adult males, belonging to low socioeconomic strata and having low educational level. The incidents occurred mainly during night at the time of power failure. The type, distribution and characteristic of the injuries suggested of their accidental nature."[2]

Reportedly, three people died during the reporting periods:

> ...one man died falling off a rooftop fleeing from what he thought was the Monkey Man, and a pregnant woman fell down stairs and died panicking as well. A third man also fell off a rooftop, running in fear when he heard another man nearby panicking, shrieking in the darkness that something had pulled on his sheets as he tried to sleep.[3]

During the reporting period, various explanations were suggested, including a rogue monkey, a half-monkey creature, an evil spirit, a robot, "a computerized creature who someone is operating with remote control," and a terrorist who was using the panic, confusion, and police reaction as a cover for some assassination.[4] However, the incident is now considered a case of mass hysteria, with the aforementioned study noting that the incident met all the criteria for a case:

- Sudden onset of dramatic symptoms with both rapid spread and rapid recovery;
- A triggering stimulant identified by the victim as a toxic gas or chemical, bugbites or environmental pollutants;
- Victims who were not sick until they see another victim become ill;
- Underlying psychological or physical stress that can be caused by hot weather, crowding, boredom or other factors[5]; and
- Victims' perceived lack of emotional and social support.[6]

The monkey-man of New Delhi is not alone in being considered a case of mass hysteria: other examples include Spring-heeled Jack from London in the nineteenth century; the Phantom Slasher of Taiwan, who allegedly attacked women and children in 1956; and continued reports of "phantom clowns" around the world.[7]

Jirmu

The Andaman Islands are an archipeologo in the Indian Ocean. The Indian union territory of the Andaman and Nicobar Islands consists of an astounding 572 islands, of which 38 are inhabited. The Andaman Islands are home to the Andamanese, a group of indigenous people that includes a number of tribes, including the Jarawa and Sentinelese tribes. Some islands can be visited from the mainland with permits; others are off-limits by law. The Sentinelese, in particular, are considered an "uncontacted tribe" that is hostile to visitors.

Great Andaman is the main archipelago of the Andaman Islands, comprising seven major islands. Throughout these islands, reports from Indigenous tribes tell of a "huge animal" in the jungles, as reported by English social anthropologist A. R. Radcliffe Brown. In the book *The Andaman Islanders* (1922), he reports:

> Throughout the Great Andaman there is a belief in a huge animal that haunts the jungles, or that haunted them in the days of the ancestors. In the North Andaman this beast is called Ĵirmu. In the days of the ancestors it is supposed to have lived at Ulibi-taŋ, where it attacked and killed any men and women who came in its way. No detailed legend about the Ĵirmu was obtained...When elephants were first introduced into the Andamans for the use of the Forest Department, they were named Uču by the natives, and have ever since retained that name. Similarly the natives of the Northern tribes call them Ĵirmu.[8]

Little else has been reported about this creature. It is unknown if this is still a strongly held belief by the Indigenous tribes of Great Andaman.

Kallana

India is home to 30,000 elephants of various subspecies, notably the Indian elephant. In the southern state of Kerala, an estimated 3,054 elephants roam. However, there could be more, as there are reports from the local Kani tribe that a dwarf species of elephants lives in the rainforests of the state.

For many years members of the Kani tribe, who live in the Western Ghat forests in Thiruvananthapuram district, have told of a dwarf-sized elephant variety that lives in the Peppara-Agastyarkoodam forest range.[9] The name "Kallana" comes from the species' preference for rocky terrain and higher altitudes, with "Kallu" meaning stones or boulders, and "aana," which means elephant. The tribe insists that Kallana are different from the common Indian elephant, which also inhabits the forests.[10]

According to the Kanis, these elephants grow up to be only five feet tall at adulthood, in contrast to the much larger Indian elephant, which reaches a height of eight or nine feet. They are able to negotiate the rocky terrains with agility and dart through the forests with much greater speed than Indian elephants.

In 2005, wildlife photographer Sali Palode, accompanied by Kani tribesman Mallan Kani, claimed to have photographed one such dwarf elephant. "I have accompanied Kani tribespeople and have seen the Kallana as far back as 1985," Sali told *New Indian Express*. "In 2005, we spotted a herd of five but managed to get a picture of only one. Again another photograph was snapped in 2010."[11] Without scientific study, it cannot be ascertained whether the reported animal is a separate (sub)species or lone members of the Indian elephant population that have genetic differences.

It is worth noting that pygmy elephants are known to exist in Asia with the Borneo elephant, a subspecies of the Asian elephant. However, Borneo elephants are still 8.2-9.8 feet tall.[12] The Borneo elephant was only recently designated a distinct subspecies, with DNA evidence proving that these elephants were isolated about three hundred thousand years ago from their cousins on mainland Asia.

Mande Barung

In northeastern India, reports have appeared of yet another Sasquatch-type creature, this one that goes by Mande Barung ("forest man") – although, due to the proximity to Nepal, some use the term "yeti." Reports center in the remote West Garo Hills in the state of Meghalaya, which borders Bangladesh.[13] The creature is reported to be black or gray and stands about ten feet (three meters) tall.[14] Most reports state that the creature is herbivorous, although some have stated that the creature eats freshwater crabs; Richard Freeman of the Centre for Fortean Zoology reported in *Adventures in Cryptozology* (2019) that his expedition found footprints near crabs that had been eaten.[15]

One of the most well-known sightings occurred in Balphakram National Park, famous for its jungle-filled canyon, diverse fauna and flora, and its treacherous descent. In April 2002, forestry officer James Marak and fourteen other officials who were carrying out a census of tigers reported that they saw what they thought was a "yeti."[16]

In 2008, "yeti" hair was analyzed in the United Kingdom by Ian Redmond, a wildlife biologist and ape conservation expert, award-winning primatologist Anna Nekaris, and microscopy expert Jon Wells at Oxford Brookes University.[17] The hair sample did not match that of any identified species and, according to Redmond, matched the cuticle pattern of the hair sample brought back to the UK by Sir Edmund Hillary after climbing Everest.[18]

Redmond and Freeman both suggested that the animal could be closely related to *Gigantopithecus blacki*, an extinct species of ape that lived in southern China three hundred thousand years ago. Very little is known about *G. blacki* due to a lack of skeletal remains, which makes it difficult to identify height and other features to make a comparison to the Mande Barung and other hominid cryptids.

CHAPTER 4
INDONESIA

Orang Pendek

KERINCI SEBLAT NATIONAL PARK, Sumatra's largest national park, hosts a wide variety of rare and endangered animals, including the Sumatran tiger, the leopard cat, Sumatran dhole, Sumatran rhinoceros, Sumatran elephant, Malayan tapir, and the sun bear. The park has hosted its share of secrets, such as the Sumatran ground cuckoos, first recorded in 1916 and not seen again until 1997, and the Sumatran muntjac, a deer rediscovered in 2002, seventy years after its original discovery. A haven for wildlife and protected from the logging that much of Sumatra suffers from, it comes as no surprise that many suspect that more animals possibly live undiscovered in the area. Reports of a mysterious primate have proliferated from a wide variety of sources, including local villagers, Dutch colonists, and scientists.

While exact details of the creature can vary, Debbie

Martyr, a researcher who has worked in Indonesia to protect the tiger population in the area, describes the creature as:

> ...usually no more than 85 or 90 [centimeters] in height – although occasionally as large as 1 [meter] 20 [centimeters]. The body is covered in a coat of dark grey or black flecked with grey hair. But it is the sheer physical power of the orang pendek that most impresses the Kerinci villagers. They speak in awe of its broad shoulders, huge chest, and upper abdomen and powerful arms. The animal is so strong, the villagers would whisper that it can uproot small trees and even break rattan vines. The legs, in comparison, are short and slim, the feet neat and small, usually turned out at an angle of up to 45 degrees. The head slopes back to a distinct crest – similar to the gorilla – and there appears to be a bony ridge above the eyes. But the mouth is small and neat, the eyes are set wide apart and the nose is distinctly humanoid. When frightened, the animal exposes its teeth – revealing oddly broad incisors and prominent, long canine teeth.[1]

Local villagers have several names for the creature, including Uhang Pandak (local Kerinci dialect), Sedapa, and Umang, among numerous other instances of the primate in the various dialects of the surrounding areas. The creature has also been referred to as Ebu Gogo, a name shared by another Indonesia crypto-primate. The creature has been reported all over Sumatra, possibly indicating a wide distribution range or several various smaller populations. However, reports most often come from Kerinci.[2] The creature is often reported to be a ground-dwelling, mostly herbivorous, bipedal animal that feeds on ginger roots, insects, river crabs, and, according to various reports, crops including corn and potatoes.

The orang pendek is generally regarded as one of the cryptids most likely to be discovered, due to the remote, undisturbed nature of Kerinci Seblat National Park, as well as the plethora of firsthand accounts and the primate's similarity to the extinct species *Homo floresiensis*. *H. floresiensis*, a human predecessor that stood at approximately 1.1 meters (3 feet, 7 inches), is known to have been present in Indonesia.[3] Henry Gee, senior editor at *Nature* magazine, speculated that the creature may have survived into the modern era, aided by the vast protected wildernesses of Sumatra and Indonesia. Richard Bert, one of the researchers who discovered the *H. floresiensis* fossils, also hinted at the possibility of the species surviving into modern times, citing local legends:

> Do the Ebu Gogo still exist? It would be a hoot to search the last pockets of rainforest on the island. Not many such pockets exist, but who knows. At the very least, searching again for that lava cave, or others like it, should be done, because remains of hair only a few hundred years old, would surely survive, snagged on

the cave walls or incorporated in deposits, and would be ideal for ancient DNA analyses.[4]

Furthermore, Dr. David Chivers, a primate biologist from the University of Cambridge, compared a cast found by three British men, Adam Davies, Andrew Sanderson, and Keith Townley, in Kerinciwith with those from other known primates and local animals and stated:

> ...the cast of the footprint taken was definitely an ape with a unique blend of features from gibbon, orangutan, chimpanzee, and human. From further examination, the print did not match any known primate species and I can conclude that this points towards there being a large unknown primate in the forests of Sumatra.[5]

Hans Brunner, an Australian hair analyst, compared the hairs to those of other primates and local animals and suggested that they originated from a previously undocumented species of primate.[6]

Several other explanations exist for the orang pendek if the unknown primate or extant *H. Floresiensis* theories are to be discredited. Researchers have suggested sun bears and gibbons, both native to the area, as possible explanations for the orang pendek sightings. Some have also suggested an extant population of orangutans, which have long been considered extinct in the area. However, very few eyewitnesses report orange hair on the orang pendek.[7]

Veo

In *The Beasts That Hide from Man*, Dr. Karl Shuker describes the veo, from the Indonesian island of Rintja, as such:

> At least 10 feet long, the veo has a long head, huge claws, and is covered dorsally and laterally with large overlapping scales, but has hair upon its head, throat, belly, lower legs, and the ends of its tail. If threatened, it will rear up on its hind legs and slash its antagonist with the formidable claws on its forepaws.[8]

Dr. Shuker cites zoologist Pierre Pfeiffer's *Bivouacs a Borneo* with recorded claims of the veo from residents of Rintja.

Cryptozoologists have noted a similarity to pangolins (scaly anteaters). The extinct Asian giant pangolin (*Manis palaeojavanicus*) of Java and Borneo, which grew to over eight feet long according to excavations, has been suggested as the source of the veo reports.[9] Dr. Shuker suggests that the veo may be a remnant population.[10]

Ahool

Reported for centuries by the Sudanese Muslims of Java, the ahool is a cryptid giant bat known for its particular sound from which it derives its name.[11] It is said to be dark grey, with a flat face that resembles that of a primate.[12]

The only reports from a Westerner come from naturalist Dr. Ernest Bartels. He first reported seeing the creature in 1925 in the Salak Mountains when a bat-like creature flew over his head. In 1927, he reported hearing the creature's distinct call from his home near Java's Tjidjenkol River, although he did not physically see the creature that night.[13] He went on to write an article in *Fate* magazine alongside Ivan T. Sanderson regarding the sightings and speculation on the nature of the creature.[14] However, his reports seem to be the last sighting of the creature.

Orang-bati

Coming from the island of Seram are reports of a "Man-Bat," described as "resembling orangutans with leathery wings or even as red, furry, flying monkeys."[15] According to local folklore, the Orang-bati abducts children and takes them to the dormant volcano Mount Kairatu.[16] Author Robert Benjamin reports a case where an English missionary by the name of Tyson Hughes heard reports of the creature, although I could not verify any report from Hughes on the matter.[17] If it is ever verified, this seems to be the only Western report of the creature. Researchers, such as Dr. Karl Shuker, have speculated that reports of the creature are that of a giant bat, larger than the current record-holder, the flying fox.[18]

Row

In Charles Miller's 1939 book *Cannibal Caravan*, the author recounts an encounter with a creature referred to by the Indigenous population as the row due to the creature's roars (described as "as close to a hiss as a roar could be.") Miller expresses an interest in venturing into the jungle to find the creature after seeing a "tusk" of the animal. Despite reservations from the local Indigenous people, Miller gathers a party. After a trek across a cliff and a plateau, Miller encounters the creature in a marshy area between two unnamed plateaus. It is described as:

> ...a light brown yellow in color...I noticed that it was covered with scales laid on like armor plate, that the plates were uneven, almost as though they were designed for camouflage...Twice more the row reared up, giving me a good view of the bony flange around its head and the projecting plates along its backbone.[19]

As they prepare to leave after the creature departs, one of the natives notes that there are more of the creatures, and Miller comments that "rifles were about as useful as citronella" against the creature.

While a fantastic story, it is unlikely that there is any truth to Miller's story. It's difficult to even verify the existence of Charles Miller, as little information about him is verifiable – aside from the fact that he is listed as the writer of two books, *Cannibal Caravan* and *Black Borneo*. The former has an introduction (written by a "L. L. Stevenson") detailing Miller's life, but little of it is verifiable. Many of Miller's adventures described in *Cannibal Caravan* are unlikely, such as joining in on a cannibal feast.

Likewise, there have been no findings of a cannibal tribe that has access to any kind of unusual tusk or plate that could come from an unknown animal. Miller's comparison of the creature to those in *The Lost World* or *King Kong* in conjunction with the description of the animal – which liberally borrows characteristics from several unrelated dinosaur species – leads to the conclusion that the creature and the events described in *Cannibal Caravan* are little more than an imaginative tale.

Javan Tiger

The Javan tiger, once identified as its own subspecies but now acknowledged as an island population of *Panthera tigris sondaica*, was last officially spotted in 1979, although it was not formally declared extinct by the IUCN until 2008.[20] The species suffered from a loss of habitat due to extensive rice farming to feed a growing twentieth-century population, as well as hunting and poisoning by farmers.[21] Several surveys have been conducted to find any record of the subspecies, but they have so far netted only "no tigers, few prey, and lots of poachers."[22]

Despite the lack of success with scientific surveys, locals and visitors alike have reported seeing or even photographing the tiger subspecies or finding evidence of its existence. One 2008 article attributes the death of a female hiker in Mount Merbabu National Park to tigers in the vicinity, with witnesses claiming that the hiker's body had been partially eaten and with locals saying that tigers live in the area.[23] Two years later, near Mount Merapi, alleged tiger footprints were found after the volcano erupted. Due to the eruption, these reports were not followed up on, and the idea was discredited by the head of the nearby national park.[24]

Alleged photos and videos of the tiger also exist. In 2016, a supposed photograph of the tiger went viral in Indonesia. In the photo, taken from above, a tiger is shown walking down a small path in a forested area. Iwan Kurniawan, the project manager of Javan Langur Center in Batu, doubted the authenticity of the photograph, commenting, "In general, the forest of Mt. Arjuno is in a bad condition. Many habitats of wildlife [have] been [destroyed] and converted into farms. It is quite impossible for a tiger to live there."[25] Indonesian nonprofit PROFAUNA stated that they planned to conduct a field check in the area that the picture allegedly shows.[26] In personal correspondence, PROFAUNA has stated that the photo was taken in captivity at the Safari Park and shows a Sumatran tiger.[27] A set of photographs and a video in 2017 spurred reports from the *New York Times* and *Smithsonian Magazine*, as well as a field investigation by the World Wildlife Fund.[28] The allegations that the animal in the video is a Javan tiger were disputed by Wulan Pusparini, a tiger expert at the Wildlife Conservation Society, who said it more closely resembles a rare Javan leopard.

Could the forests of Java be hiding the presumed extinct Javan tiger? Many animals in the area can go for years without being spotted, such as the aforementioned Javan leopard. Perhaps the tiger remains critically endangered in the dense vastness of the jungle.

CHAPTER 5

JAPAN

Akkorokamui

ACCORDING TO THE AINU PEOPLE, the indigenous people of the lands surrounding the Sea of Okhotsk, a giant water-based creature lives in Uchiura Bay on Hokkaido Island, Japan's second largest island. The creature is commonly known as the Akkorokamui, although the name given to it by the Ainu people is Atkor Kamuy. It is generally described as resembling an octopus of tremendous size, similar to the kraken of Norway sailor folklore. However, the few researchers of the Akkorokamui have also suggested that the creature could also be a squid or jellyfish of a colossal size, including suggestions that it could be the mysterious but very real giant squid (*Architeuthis dux*).

In Ainu folklore, Akkorokamui is both feared for its sheer power and acknowledged as a water deity, specifically as the lord of Uchiura Bay.[1] The word "kamuy" in its Aimu name is an Ainu term for a divine being.

Yokai.com, the illustrated database of Japanese folk-lore, tells the origin story of the Akkorokamui as such:

> Long ago, in the mountains near the village of Rebunge, there lived a gigantic spider named Yaushikep. Yaushikep was enormous. His great red body stretched over one hectare in area. One day, Yaushikep descended from the mountains and attacked the people of Rebunge. He shook the earth as he rampaged, destroying everything in his path. The villagers were terrified. They prayed to the gods to save them. The god of the sea, Repun Kamuy, heard their prayers and pulled Yaushikep into the bay. When the great spider was taken into the water, he transformed into a giant octopus, and took over charge of the bay as its god.

The Akkorokamui is said to be a gigantic octopus-like or squid-like creature, reaching sizes of up to 110 meters in length and with a coloration that is said to be a striking, brilliant red. Legends says that the creature can be seen from great distances due to its enormous size and coloration.[2] Much like the Norwegian kraken, the Akkorokamui is said to attack ships, and Ainu fishermen have been known to bring scythes to protect their boats.[3]

In addition to the beliefs of the Ainu people, the creature has also reportedly been sighted by visitors to the island as well. An account from a Japanese fisherman in the nineteenth century, translated by researcher Brent Swancer:

And I saw ahead something huge and red undulating under the waves. I at first thought my eyes deceived me and that I was merely seeing the reflection of sun upon the water, but as I approached, I could see that in fact it was an enormous monster, 80 meters in length at least, with large, thick tentacles as big around as a man's torso. The thing fixed me with a huge, staring eye before sinking out of sight into the depths.[4]

The nineteenth-century Englishman and missionary John Batchelor, who lived among the Ainu for some time, wrote a journal entry of an alleged incident concerning an Akkorokamui in his book *The Ainu and their Folklore*, where he writes:

On inquiring about the matter in the morning we found the whole village under a cloud. Three men, it was said, were out trying to catch a sword-fish, when all at once a great sea-monster, with large staring eyes, appeared in front of them and proceeded to attack the boat. A desperate fight ensued. The monster was round in shape, and emitted a dark fluid which had a very powerful and noxious odour. The three men fled in dismay, not so much indeed for fear, they say, but on account of the dreadful smell. However that may have been, they were so scared that the next morning all three refused to get up and eat; they were lying in their beds pale and trembling...The chief himself told me that he was holding a grand consultation with his men that very day at noon to consider the matter. Prayers would have to be said...The men say it was a devil; and I am inclined to think from the description that it was really a "devil-fish" or octopus.[5]

Keen readers will note the description of the creature emitting a "dark fluid," as an octopus might.

Brent Swancer compiled several twentieth-century reports of the creature:

> The passengers of one cruise ship in the bay in the 1980s were met with the surprising sight of what appeared to be a massive creature thrashing about in the water with what appeared to be tentacles breaking the surface. The creature was described as being bright red in color and being around 80 feet in diameter. A fishing boat in the 70s also reported bumping up against something in the water which they at first took to be a rock, but when the crew looked overboard they saw an enormous red mass, and according to the report an eye peering out from the depths that was supposedly the size of a dinner plate. There was even a report of a beachcomber who supposedly came across a piece of what he said was an octopus tentacle that was reported as being around as thick as a telephone pole. It is unclear what happened to this specimen.[6]

As to the identity of the creature, the description (and the note about the "dark fluid") suggests an oversized octopus. The largest known octopus is the giant Pacific octopus (*Enteroctopus dofleini*) and is found in the northern Pacific Ocean near Japan. These creatures have arm spans of up to 3 to 5 meters (9.75 to 16 feet), with some reports of larger specimens. However, the giant Pacific octopus is most often found at two hundred meters in the sea, so an appearance in Uchiura Bay would be unusual. Additionally, the giant Pacific octopus, despite being quite large, is still miniscule in comparison to the titanic size reported for the Akkorokamui. In fact, if the reported size of the Akkorokamui is anywhere close to true, it would surpass the size of the largest animal known to exist, the blue whale. In all likelihood, the creature's size has been exaggerated for various reasons.

Swancer suggested that the creature could be a giant squid (*Architeuthis dux*) or a granrojo (big red) jellyfish (*Tiburonia granrojo*); however, both of these creatures reside in waters far deeper than Uchiura Bay.[7]

Giant Snake of Mount Tsurugi

The Giant Snake of Mount Tsurugi was reported once, in 1973, wherein four forestry workers reported seeing a massive, thirty-three-foot-long snake with shiny black scales.[8] The workers stated that the creature made chirping noises at them, as if to warn them away. According to Brad Steiger, the workers brought back "hundreds" of volunteers, who were unable to find the snake but found marks left by its coils, which measured sixteen inches wide, as well as trees allegedly knocked over by the giant animal.[9]

Mount Tsurugi, on the border of Miyoshi, Mima and Naka in Tokushima Prefecture, has spiritual significance in the region and is also one of the centers of Shugendō, a combination sect of Shintoism and Buddhism. Additionally, there is allegedly a legend stating that the mountain is actually a man-made pyramid and contains the treasures of King Solomon.[10] However, I could not find any information on this legend from Japanese sources. I also was unable to verify if a photograph of a skull, alleged to be from a giant snake, came from a local history museum, as reported by several blogs.

Hibagon

The hibagon is Japan's equivalent to Sasquatch. The creature reportedly lives near Hiroshima in Hibayama National Park and has been sighted since the 1970s. Like other cryptid apes, the hibagon is said to be bipedal and hairy, with a height around five feet tall.[11] The creature was consistently described as being like a gorilla and "a face shaped like an inverted triangle."[12] The creature is named for the Hiba mountain in the town of Shobara (formerly Saijo), where the sightings took place in the early 1970s.[13]

"Hibagon fever" took over the town, which is located in the northern part of the Hiroshima Prefecture. Reporters from around the world interviewed residents, while the town created a post to handle the "issue of anthropoid apes" (the person in charge of that post previously dealt with taxes in the city). The town government addition created a unique policy to pay 5,000 yen (equivalent to ¥16,103.03 yen in 2021, or just over $100USD) for each resident who spotted the creature. The money was to "make up for inconvenience" caused by a hibagon sighting. By October 1974, the town office had received twenty-nine reports about hibagon appearing in the wild. Sightings stopped by June 1975, at which point the town declared that "hibagon fever" was over.[14] However, depictions of the hibagon were still common around the town.

The hibagon has not attracted much study since its heyday in the 1970s. A rumor that existed at the time was that the hibagon was an escaped gorilla from Asa Zoo in the city of Hiroshima, which is ninety kilometers from Saijo. Some residents thought the hibagon was a warning against recreational facilities that were under construction in the area, including camping grounds. "The god of Hiba mountain sent hibagon to haunt us," one person was cited as saying.[15] Janet Bord's *Alien Animals* presents several additional theories, including that the hibagon was a deserter from the Japanese Army hiding in the wilderness, or even that the creature was a mutant caused by the use of nuclear weapons in Hiroshima, citing "some investigators."[16] I was unable to find Japanese sources making these claims.

Issie

While the Loch Ness Monster of Scotland has a hold on the West's imagination regarding lake monsters, Japan has two lake monsters of its own: Issie and Kussie, both named after Nessie.

Issie-kun, as the creature is affectionately known,[17] has been part of Japanese folklore for several centuries. Folklore states that Issie (sometimes Isshi) was a white mare whose foal was stolen by a samurai. In despair, Issie threw herself into Lake Ikeda and became a lake monster who occasionally surfaces to look for her lost foal.[18]

The creature grew to its status as Japan's most famous cryptid when, in 1978, twenty people reported seeing several black humps several meters in length moving through the water. Later that same year, a man named Toshiaki Matsuhara caught what is alleged to be the creature in several black-and-white photographs.[19] Additionally, in 1991, a visitor allegedly captured the creature on video – the witness estimated that the creature was ninety-eight feet in length.[20] Other descriptions range from sixteen feet to ninety feet.[21]

Lake Ikeda is the largest volcanic lake in Kyushu and has a depth of up to 233 meters, which gives the water an intense ocean-blue color.[22] Notably, the lake is known for its giant eels, which can grow up to six feet in length.[23]

Kussie

Kusshii, or Kussie, is another lake monster that allegedly resides in Hokkaidō's Lake Kussharo. Hokkaidō is the second largest of Japan's islands; Lake Kussharo is Japan's sixth largest lake, and like Issie's Lake Ikeda, it is a caldera lake and freezes over in the winter months.

Unlike Issie, Kussie is usually described as eel-like, in contrast to Issie's association with plesiosaurs.[24] Sightings for the creature were first reported and peaked in the 1970s. The first known sighting occurred on September 2, 1973, in which Toshio Komama took a distant picture of two creatures in the lake.[25] Another sighting occurred on September 18, 1973, in which one person saw a "50-foot animal with ridges along its back." The animal was described as moving "swiftly" and creating a wake.[26] *Newsweek* reported a firefighter seeing the creature in 1997, although this appears to be the most recent report of the creature.[27]

Tsuchinoko

The tsuchinoko (ツチノコ or 槌の子), literally translating to "child of hammer," is a snakelike creature that originates in Japanese folklore. The creature has over fifty names across Japan, but the description largely remains the same, with the creature being between thirty and eighty centimetres (twelve and thirty-one inches) in length, similar in appearance to a snake, but with a central girth that is much wider than its head or tail, and as having fangs and venom similar to that of a viper.[28] Various reports include folkloric elements, such as that it can roll like a wheel by eating its tail and that it can leap up to three feet.[29] However, these additions to descriptions of the creature do not seem to have carried into the twentieth century and beyond.

A live Tsuchinoko was reportedly captured in Mikata, Hyogo prefecture, in June 1969 by a M. Tokutake. He supposedly captured it with a forked stick and kept it for a couple of days before deciding to eat it for inexplicable reasons. He does not seem to have commented on the taste.[30] Another live specimen was reportedly captured in Mikata on June 6, 2000, with it allegedly put on display in a glass box in the city's visitor center. Researcher Brent Swancer, who lives in Japan, could not find what became of the specimen. He suggested that it could have been a hoax put on by the town to drum up interest in their annual tsuchinoko hunt, which attracts people from all over the country and boasts a reward of over a million yen to anyone who finds proof of the creature.[31]

Several alleged specimens have been found to be common snakes from Japan. Conventional researchers tend to explain the tsuchinoko sightings as snakes that have recently fed, which would explain the stomach bulge.[32] If one discounts the folkloric elements of the creature, the explanation seems like a good fit.

CHAPTER 6
MALAYSIA

Orang Mawas

IN THE JUNGLES of the Malaysian state of Johor, there are reports of another hairy primate, referred to as the orang mawas, or *hantu jarang gigi* – "snaggle-toothed ghost."[1] The creature is reported to be 2.4–3 meters (approximately 7.8–9 feet) tall and bipedal, much like a larger form of the American Sasquatch.[2] Vincent Chow, a Malaysian cryptozoologist that has collected reports of the creature, reports that the creature has chimp-like ears.[3] In 1995, a set of tracks with four toes was found, although it was never verified as being that of an orang mawas. Another set of tracks in 2013 was found to be that of a tapir.[4]

Gregory Forth notes in *Images of the Wildman in Southeast Asia* that the term "mawas" is imported from the native languages of Sumatra, where it is used to refer to orangutans. Forth notes that this may indicate a mythologization of the term from cultural memory.[5] Other skeptic observations compare the creature, as with many other Oceania primates, to a possible misidentification of the Malaysian sun bear. However, Chow's collection of "chimp-like" ears, as well as the noted bipedal nature of reports, contradict that explanation. The reports could be of a known monkey or possibly an extant local population of orangutans. Due to the height of the creature, some have suggested that the creature is a remnant population of the *Gigantopithecus*, a genus of ape that went extinct one hundred thousand years ago.

Cigau

Deep in the jungles of Sumatra lies, allegedly, a species of golden big cats.[6] Incredibly rare, much like the scientifically accepted Sumatran tiger, the cats are described as smaller than the local Sumatran tiger population with a prominent golden colour, as well as a ruff of fur with no spots or stripes.[7] Notably, the description is closer to that of a lion, particularly that of the endangered Indian Asiatic lion, than the remaining tiger population. Of particular note, the cigau is also said to have front legs higher than its hind legs, a trait commonly associated with prehistoric cats, such as the saber-toothed cat.[8] It is said to be aggressive and allegedly frequents the wilderness area east of Mount Kerinci.[9]

Some early native reports are of the particularly fantastical variety. George M. Eberhart notes that some descriptions describe a creature "half tiger, half ape."[10] However, this is not indicative of more recent reports and seems limited to early reports, possibly to scare early colonizers. Richard Freeman of the Centre for Fortean Zoology recounts an eyewitness report that was told to him on a 2003 expedition:

> In the dead of night the cigau came from the forest to claim him. It stalked right into their camp and dragged him off into the darkness. It was smaller but stockier than a tiger. It had a silvery lion-like mane and golden fur. Its forelegs were longer than its back legs like the build of a hyena. It had a short, tufted, cow-like tail. The men searched the jungle franticly for their lost comrade but when they found him he was minus a stomach, disemboweled by the cigau. It would be easy to dismiss the cigau as a piece of folklore, the wrath of the jungle sent to punish transgressors, but if you recall similar attributes are given to the very real tiger; for example, the tiger becoming angry at those who go naked in the forest. Sahar's father also spoke of a cigau who laired near a fallen tree that formed a natural bridge over a river. It would swim out and devour those who slipped into the water. Debbie also commented that she had many recent reports of the cigau in water. Most of them mentioned it flinging back its mane to shake off the water.[11]

CHAPTER 7

MONGOLIA

Almas

LIKE MOST CULTURES of the world, the Mongolians have a wildman figure, generally known as the almas (Mongolian: Алмас). The creature is said to inhabit the Caucasus and Pamir Mountains of Central Asia and the Altai Mountains of western Mongolia. The almas is consistently described as a large, humanlike bipedal creature between five and six and a half feet tall. The almas is covered in thick, dark brown, reddish brown, yellowish, or black hair all over its body except for its hands and face, though they often have thick beards as well. Both male and female almas have been reported.[1] Like the North American Bigfoot, the almas is described as having large feet.

Researcher Nathan Wenzel, who investigated legends of the almas in the eastern regions of Mongolia, gives the following description based on reports from across the region:

According to the legends, the almas lives in the caves of remote, mountainous regions. Due to its strong, stocky body, the almas has incredible running, climbing, and swimming abilities, though some are afraid of water. The almas, like humans, is an omnivore with a wide diet consisting of anything from raw meat of small or large animals to fresh fruit or vegetables or even tree roots. Many of the legends also imply that the almas is nocturnal, as many of the stories occur at dusk or after nightfall. The almas' presence is often announced to people by its distinct, very strong, foul odor. They are also known to scream very loudly and distinctively. Almases normally appear alone and are solitary creatures. In many legends, female almases are even more dangerous and fierce than males whenever they or their children are threatened, and they often are portrayed with a strong maternal instinct.[2]

Regarding the location of the creature, Wenzel writes:

The legends of the almas usually occur in a very specific location within Mongolia. Traditionally, western Mongolia, including the aimags of Khovd, Govi-Altai, and Bayan-Ulgii have been the source of nearly all of the almas legends. The Altai mountain range as well as the Tian Shen mountain pass on the border with China are fertile ground for almas legends. There have also been a much smaller number of stories emanating from the Gobi Desert region. The central and eastern parts of the country do not normally have their own almas legends in which the action takes place in their own regions...legends with a creature of the exact same description as the almas are also found in the Pamir Mountain range and even farther away in the Caucuses. People in these regions also have legends of the almas that are essentially the same as those found in Mongolia, making the legend of the almas a geographically international one.[3]

Many of these descriptions, including the foul-smelling odor, closely link to other wildman/Bigfoot stories around the world, including Sasquatch and Nepal's yeti. Wenzel compared and contrasted the almas and the yeti in his paper as such:

The yeti is found in the Himalayas and is described as larger and more ape-like than the almas...The yeti is also reportedly much larger than the almas, with a height of up to nine meters...The more ape-like yeti is also known for its cone-shaped head and sloping forehead. Like the almas, however, the yeti is known for its great strength, upright walk, hair-covered body, and large feet...Despite the opinions of some people and the fact that the almas and yeti have some characteristics in common, they are distinct even at the basic, descriptive level.[4]

Russian geographer Nikolay Przhevalsky describes the

almas, as related to him under the name *kung-guressu* ("man-beast"), as follows:

> We were told that it had a flat face like that of a human being, and that it often walked on two legs, that its body was covered with a thick black fur, and its feet armed with enormous claws; that its strength was terrible, and that not only were hunters afraid of attacking it, but that the inhabitants removed their habitations from those parts of the country which it visited.[5]

Various explanations for the almas exist, much like they do for other Sasquatch-like figures. Cryptozoologists have suggested that the creature is an unknown species of ape. Wenzel suggested that the creature could be used in folklore as a boogeyman: "The almas is concrete enough to be a monster or boogeyman, but mysterious enough to be flexible and used by different people in different situations."[6] In 1964, a Soviet scientist from the Soviet Academy of Sciences proposed that the almas could be a relict population of Neanderthals still living in Siberia.[7]

Mongolian death worm

The Mongolian death worm (Mongolian: олгой-хорхой, olgoi-khorkhoi, "large intestine worm") is a creature alleged to reside in the Gobi Desert, the sixth-largest desert in the world, which is located in northern China and southern Mongolia. The area was particularly important during the time of the Silk Road and has been home to people for centuries.

The name "large intestine worm" is said to come from the death worm's body shape, which resembles that of a cow's intestine.[8] Ivan Mackerle, who traveled to Mongolia to search for the creature many times, described the creature as such:

> Sausage-like worm over half a metre (20 inches) long, and thick as a man's arm, resembling the intestine of cattle. Its tail is short, as [if] it were cut off, but not tapered. It is difficult to tell its head from its tail because it has no visible eyes, nostrils or mouth. Its colour is dark red, like blood or salami...It moves in odd ways – either it rolls around or squirms sideways, sweeping its way about. It lives in desolate sand dunes and in the hot valleys of the Gobi Desert with saxaul plants underground. It is possible to see it only during the hottest months of the year, June and July; later it burrows into the sand and sleeps. It gets out on the ground mainly after the rain, when the ground is wet. It is dangerous, because it can kill people and animals instantly at a range of several metres.[9]

In regard to its ranged attacks, the death worm is alleged to be able to spit deadly venom at prey and, in some accounts, emit an intense electric charge.[10] It is also said to possess "spike-like projections at both ends" of its body.[11]

In his memoir, researcher and TV host Josh Gates

explains sufficiently why the creature is still sought after despite these outlandish claims:

> Even though Mongolia is one of the least densely popu-
> lated places on earth, residents scattered [across] more
> than 600,000 square miles of desert are universally
> versed in tales of the Death Worm. This is a narrative
> that has transcended distance and time, passed down
> for generations.[12]

While legends of the Mongolian death worm have existed for generations, it was only in 1926 that it began to be noticed by Western visitors. Zoologist Roy Chapman Andrews wrote in his work *On the Trail of Ancient Man*:

> This is probably an entirely mythical animal, but it may
> have some little basis in fact, for every northern Mongol
> firmly believes in it and gives essentially the same
> description. It is said to be about two feet long, the body
> shaped like a sausage, and to have no head or legs; it is
> so poisonous that even to touch it means instant death.
> It is reported to live in the most arid, sandy regions of
> the western Gobi. What reptile could have furnished
> the basis for the description is a mystery![13]

Richard Freeman, a prominent cryptozoologist, traveled to Mongolia in 2005 and says his findings were as
such:

The worm certainly exists. When we talked to people during our trip in Mongolia, they were all quite certain of that. They didn't believe it could spit electricity, but they did believe it was venomous. They're very afraid of it. A whole family packed up their tent hut and moved when they heard of sightings of the worm.

Nobody knows anyone who was killed by the worm, but there are many who say they've seen it. There's a rumour of a child who poked the worm with a stick, got spat at, and died. But it's just a story.

I think it's a reptile. It's either an unknown species of worm lizard (related to snakes) or an unknown species of sand boa. Nobody thinks of it as a mythical creature in Mongolia, but a real living animal.[14]

Similar to Freeman, investigator and writer Benjamin Radford says that a worm would be unlikely to survive in an inhospitable environment such as the Gobi Desert. He adds that, "it is likely a type of snake or legless lizard," but says that, "[being one of those species] also means it would be a vertebrate animal with a spine that would presumably be found by searchers."

The consensus among researchers such as Shuker and author Richard Freeman is that the Mongolian Death Worm likely does not exist, and the belief is instead based upon sightings of either a type of limbless reptile known as a worm lizard (which resembles a large worm, burrows underground and can reach several feet in length), or a type of sand boa snake.[15]

Freeman and others believe that the reported electric powers are exaggerated folkloric accounts, although the spitting venom could be similar to the Gila monster (*Heloderma suspectum*) of the southwestern desert regions of the United States and northwestern Mexico.

As it has been over a decade since the last major expedition, it is unknown how strong belief in the Mongolian death worm is in the reported regions. Further study could be conducted to see if increased modernization has affected the reputation of the creature.

CHAPTER 8
NEPAL

Yeti

IN THE 1957 Hammer Films production *The Abominable Snowman*, starring Peter Cushing and Forrest Tucker, an expedition is launched to find the legendary creature known as the yeti. Tucker's character, Tom Friend, is a fame seeker who is contrasted with Cushing's academic-minded Dr. John Rollason. After a series of misfortunes, Rollason meets two yeti when they come to collect their fallen comrade. Looking into the extremely human eyes of one of the yeti, Rollason realizes that the yeti are destined to one day rule the earth, and denies knowledge of finding anything upon his return to the main camp, where he is questioned by his wife and the Lama of the monastery of Rong-buk.[1]

The Abominable Snowman was just one of the many pieces of media that made their way to Westerners as the Himalayas became an object for fascination for many, owing to the "exotic" nature of the area and its people – and their belief systems.

The history of the yeti is not well recorded by Western sources. According to the traditions of the Lepcha people who are indigenous to the Himalayan region, the yeti is an ape-like glacier spirit that holds influence over the success of hunting trips.[2] There is nothing to suggest a flesh-and-blood creature, but reports from the 1800s, recorded by some of the first Western visitors to the area, do tell of locals who have seen the creature, although mystical powers are often ascribed to it.

One of the earliest Western accounts of wild men in the Himalayas came from Scottish explorer Laurence Waddell's *Among the Himalayas* (1899). Waddell writes:

Some large footprints in the snow led across our track, and away up to the higher peaks. These were alleged to be the trail of the hairy wild men who are believed to live amongst the eternal snows, along with the mythical white lions...The belief in these creatures is universal among Tibetans. None, however, of the many Tibetans I have interrogated on this subject could ever give me an authentic case. On the most superficial investigation it always resolved itself into something that somebody heard tell of. These so-called hairy wild men are evidently the great yellow snow bear...which is highly carnivorous, and often kills yaks. [3]

In 1951, noted English Himalayan explorer Eric

Shipton caught on camera footprints left behind by the yeti, which showed a thumb-like impression instead of a toe. Some propose that the prints are simply that of a Himalayan animal's prints that have been distorted by melting snow, while others hold the photographs up as one of the best pieces of evidence in support of the yeti's existence.

The first two people known to have reached the summit of Mount Everest, New Zealand mountaineer Sir Edmund Hillary and Sherpa mountaineer Tenzing Norgay, reported finding tracks on their trek. However, Hillary found reports of the yeti unreliable. Tenzing said in his first autobiography that his father had seen the creature; in spite of that, he reported being skeptical of the yeti in his follow-up book.

Reports of the yeti caught the attention of Texas-based oil heir Tom Slick, who launched several expeditions to the Himalayas to find evidence of the creature. His adventures in this regard (and other investigations he funded) are covered in depth in Loren Coleman's *Tom Slick and the Search for Yeti* (1989) and *Tom Slick: True Life Encounters in Cryptozoology* (2002). A particular interest of Slick's was the Pangboche Hand, named for the village in which it once resided. According to local tradition, a monk had discovered a yeti while searching for a place to meditate; sometime later, he returned to find the yeti deceased and took its hand and scalp. One of Slick's early expeditions resulted in a photograph of the hand, while a subsequent expedition took a decidedly unique turn: expedition member Peter Byrne took a finger from the hand after being refused access to it by the monks, aided by actor James Stewart in smuggling the bone to the United Kingdom. Byrne stated that he replaced the finger with human bones, which were subsequently analyzed by Sir Edmund Hillary and Marlin Perkins, not knowing about the replacement. Byrne gave the finger to primatologist Professor William Osman Hill, where it was rediscovered in 2008.

Tests were run on the finger, with scientists finding that it was of human origin. Dr. Rob Jones, senior scientist at the Zoological Society of Scotland, said, "We have got a very, very strong match to a number of existing reference sequences on human DNA databases...It's very similar to existing human sequences from China and that region of Asia but we don't have enough resolution to be confident of a racial identification." The finger is all that remains of the hand, as the rest was stolen in the 1990s and has allegedly been traded in underground art circles and private collections since.[4]

Sir Hillary continued his investigations into the yeti in the 1960s, notably looking for the yeti during the 1960–61 Silver Hut expedition, although that was not the primary intention for the expedition. Supported by Marlin Perkins, the director of the Lincoln Park Zoo in Chicago, the expedition focused on the Rowaling Valley due to reports. Members of the expedition set up cameras, telescopes, tripwires, and Cap-Chur guns around the Ripimu Glacier at 18,000 feet (5,500 m) feet.[5] Hillary brought back a supposed yeti scalp to Chicago; Marca Burns compared the sample to known animals such as the Himalayan serow, blue bear, and black bear and found that the sample closely resembled the serow.[6]

While an interest in the yeti remained via popular culture, field expeditions largely stopped by the mid-1960s. This is perhaps due to North American audiences shifting their focus to the North American Sasquatch – besides the obvious interest in a creature living undiscovered in "your backyard" (so to speak), it is much more cost-efficient for researchers to host field expeditions for the Sasquatch.

In December 2007, Josh Gates of the paranormal investigation show *Destination Truth*, which aired on SyFy from 2007 to 2012, reported that he and his team had discovered footprints while filming an episode in the Himalayas.[7] Of the three tracks found in the rocky area, the first print was described as "pristine," a right paw mark, thirty-three centimeters (thirteen inches) long, with five toes in a wide spread of twenty-five centimeters. A cast of the print was created and subsequently analyzed by Jeff Meldrum at the University of Idaho. Meldrum, a renowned anthropologist with a specialty in bipedalism, found that the cast was "too morphologically accurate" to be fake or man-made and that they were distinctly different from bear tracks. He compared the cast to another print from North America that is alleged to be from a Sasquatch, noting the similarities. The print was subsequently gifted to Disney for use at their Expedition

Everest ride, an example of the impact of the yeti in popular culture.

Sporadic reports of the yeti still occur, but none have produced the excitement and interest of the mid-1900s in finding the yeti, and certainly there are fewer reports than of similar creatures such as the Sasquatch. Like the nearby yeren and almas, it seems that many have lost interest in investigating the creature, although occasional work will be done, such as the aforementioned *Destination Truth* episode and a follow-up in 2009.

As with all hominid creatures, a variety of explanations have been suggested. As with the Sasquatch, scientists have pointed to local bear species: the Tibetan blue bear or the Himalayan brown bear, both of which are known to walk upright on occasions. Footprints and hair samples that were reported to be from the yeti have been found to be from these species, leading credence to that explanation.[8] Daniel C. Taylor published *Yeti: The Ecology of a Mystery* in 2017 that included a never-before published photograph in the archives of the Royal Geographical Society, taken in 1950 by Eric Shipton alongside his more famous photograph, that included scratches that are allegedly bear nail marks. As with the yeren, various researchers have proposed that yeti sightings are the result of a surviving population of surviving *gigantopithecines*, which went extinct three hundred thousand years ago. The idea was first put forward by zoologist Wladimir Tschernezky in a 1960 article in *Nature* about the Shipton footprints.

While fewer investigations are being conducted regarding the existence of the yeti, it still maintains a status as one of the most well-known cryptids. It's certainly the most well-known cryptid presented in this book. Media continues to feature the creature, and cryptozoology researchers and fans will continue to discuss the creature for decades to come, likely with no firm resolution.

CHAPTER 9

NEW ZEALAND

Maero and Moehau

ACCORDING TO SOME MAORI TRADITIONS, the great forests of New Zealand were once inhabited by a race of humanoids known as maero, arboreal primates with long fingernails that they used to disembowel their prey. Known to be hairy, naked, and weaponless, these creatures allegedly fled to the forests after their land was taken over and desecrated by the arrival of the Maori.[1] Such tales are reminiscent of archaeological accounts of the invasion of humans and the destruction of the Neanderthals, although the maero are often portrayed as supernatural beings. There is a resemblance in some respects between the Maori tales of the maero and primitive European beliefs concerning water-trolls, gigantic hairy beings with a taste for human flesh.

Some writers have suggested that the more modern legends of the moehau reflect a descendant of the maero, or perhaps even the same creature. Although not much is said about the maero in Maori storytelling, the creature's incredible fingernails are also present in reports of the moehau, so named for their preferred habitat at the base of Mount Moehau, one of the North Island's most distinct features.[2]

Of the explanations for the maero or moehau, researcher Robyn Gosset was told in 1970 by County Councillor J. Reddy that the moehau simply started as a joke, although this does not completely account for the eyewitness sightings and mythology that existed in the late 1800s and 1900s.[3] Some cryptozoologists have speculated that the creature is some type of known-to-science primate, such as an escaped gorilla. Some historians speculate that the maero legend may be a cultural memory or retelling of the destruction of a primitive humanoid, particularly due to its similarity to records of the extinction of the Neanderthals.

Waitoreke

Also known as the Maori otter, the waitoreke is an alleged otter from New Zealand, sometimes also described as resembling a beaver, causing some confusion. The creature is sometimes described as being as big as a cat, with short, brownish fur. Reports also give evidence of a musky smell and the ability to lay eggs, which would make the creature a monotreme like the platypus and echidna.

James Cook reported a sighting of a mammal on his initial expedition:

> For three or four days after our arrival in Pickersgill Harbour and as we were clearing the woods to set up our tents, a four-footed animal was seen by three or four of our people but as no two gave the same description of it I cannot say what kind it is. However, all agree that it was the size of a cat with short legs and a mouse colour. One of the seamen, and he who had the best view of it, said it had a bushy tail and was more like a jackal than any animal he knew. The most possible conjecture is that it is of some new species. Be that as it may, we are now certain that the country is not as destitute of quadrupeds as once thought.[4]

Early reports from 1844 referred to beavers living on the east side of Lake Wanaka, but G. A. Mantell, describing accounts of this animal by the local Maoris, concluded that "altogether the account pointed to an animal resembling the otter or badger, rather than to the beaver."[5] With the revised interest in the waitoreke in the mid-twentieth century, J. S. Watson reviewed all the available literature and concluded that "there is very little ground for any belief in the animal's existence; nevertheless a shadow of doubt remains and it would be unwise altogether to ignore the possibility however remote it may be."[6]

Reports continued into the 1970s. John Tasker records

numerous accounts up to 1957 in *Quest Aotearoa –
Volume One.*[7] G. A. Pollock suggested in 1974 that the
survival of the creature, if it ever existed, is unlikely given
the drop-off in sightings, although he points to the isolated
Waipori swamp on the Taieri plain as a possible place for
the creature to remain hidden.[8]

A variety of explanations for the creature have been
suggested – the most obvious, of course, being a population
of otters in New Zealand. There exist several explanations
for how a population of otters would develop in New
Zealand, including a possible population of the hairy-
nosed otter or a wayward population of sea otters.[9]
Bernard Heuvelmans and, indeed, even Charles Darwin,
have suggested an evolutionary pattern from the creature;
as Heuvelmans describes, this discovery would have
profound scientific consequences: "paleogeographical
reconstructions would have to be completely revised and
the date of submergence of certain continental bridges
[between Australia and New Zealand] would have to be
changed by several tens of millions of years."[10] Darwin said
of the animal, should one be found it might "turn out something like the Solnhofen bird [*Archaeopteryx*]," which clar-
ified the evolution of dinosaurs to birds.[11]

Additional explanations exist, including the popular
freshwater otter theory. German author and theorist
Wilhelm Bölsche suggested that the creature could be a
type of proto-mammal.[12]

Hakawai

The Hakawai is a notable, most likely solved mystery, a preserved memory of two extinct creatures. The bird was described by a Ngāti Apa chief to the governor of New Zealand Sir George Grey as:

> Its colour was red and black and white. It was a bird of (black) feathers, tinged with yellow and green; it had a bunch of red feathers on the top of its head. It was a large bird, as large as the moa.[13]

Grey noted in a speech before Parliament that this legend is seemingly confirmed by the discovery of the Haast's eagle, a bird that went extinct after the moa, its primary source of food, died out due to overhunting.[14]

Researcher C. M. Miskelly conducted extensive research in his paper "The Identity of the Hakawai," published in 1987. Miskelly compared the reported distribution and the decline in reports to a few islands of the Hakawai with the South Island snipe, a formally recognized bird that is now classified as extinct. Miskelly followed an astounding convergence in the reports and even confirmed that the calls of the reported Hakawai were comparable to that of the South Island snipe. With that, the Hakawai has entered the New Zealand lexicon as an alternate name for the extinct snipe.[15]

Kumi Lizard

It is truly no secret that people may try to lend credence to a rumour by tying in someone of particular credibility. In terms of New Zealand cryptozoology, a particular rumor going around is that Captain James Cook, the first Westerner on the island, was told of a particularly large reptile named the Kumi lizard. Many of the articles that state that Cook was informed about the Kumi lizard cite the 1970 edition of *New Zealand Mysteries* by Robyn Jenkin.[16] This was later removed in the 1996 edition of the book, likely due to the lack of verification available for the rumour.

Regardless of the Cook legend, the Kumi lizard has a long history as a monitor alleged to live in New Zealand, often habituating trees. The animal is said to resemble the extinct monitor *Megalania* of Australia, though significantly smaller at 1.5 meters (4.9 feet) in comparison to *Megalania*'s 4.5 to 7 meters (15–23 feet).

An early report of the creature reports it as having six legs. According to one Hugh Carleton in 1875, the creature was captured, presumably by natives. When Carleton went to the office of James Hector to report the capture, he returned to the point of capture to find the creature hacked into pieces by the horrified Maori.[17] A more common report of the creature occurred in September 1898 and was reported by W. D. Lysnar's East Coast station, Arowhana. According to the account, a Maori bushman spotted a huge lizard (five feet in length) approaching him before veering off into a rata tree. Lysnar and the rest of the party photographed footprints in the bush, but could not find the animal. By all accounts these photos have never surfaced, if they ever existed.[18] Reverend J. W. Stack reported hearing stories from the Maori regarding lizards two to three feet in length referred to as *uru ngarara* that burrowed on the Canterbury Plains.[19]

In 1994, an excavation of the Earnscleugh Cave, near Alexandra in Central Otago, was conducted.[20] The cave was originally discovered in the 1870s by a father and son who discovered neck bones of the extinct moa. Bones found in initial investigations include bones of three extinct birds, the moa (*Dinornis giganteus*), a New Zealand goose (*Cnemiornis calcitrans*), and a duck species (*Euryanas finschi*), as well as various other species. Original excavations in 1899 recorded the findings of a lower jaw and a rib bone of a large lizard, which was suggested to be from a Kumi lizard. However, the jaw is now lost, and the rib bone was not examined by scientists of the time. Its whereabouts are also unknown.[21]

While reports of the Kumi lizard significantly dropped off after the start of the twentieth century, Ted Rye, while working at the Karapiro Hydro Works, described an encounter with two animals feeding on a dead opossum. According to Jenkin's telling of the encounter, the animals looked "like overgrown guinea pigs with glossy, smooth coats of a dark-brown or black colour" with no tails. While the description doesn't perfectly align with previous descriptions of the Kumi lizard, the description can be blamed on the darkness at the time of the encounter.

Reports of the Kumi lizard have largely died out since the start of the twentieth century. One could speculate this as a reduction in the population of the creatures (or even extinction) as the population of humans in New Zealand rapidly expands into its native lands, or that interest in the creature has died and been relegated to folklore of previous generations.

Kawekaweau

The story of the kawekaweau is a curious one. The animal was elusive even in the late 1800s. In 1871, Walter Buller wrote: "The kawekaweau, a beautiful striped lizard, sometimes attaining a length of two feet, is still undescribed. It was formerly abundant in the forests north of Auckland and is still occasionally spotted. F. E. Maning, of Hokianga, recently obtained possession of a pair of live ones, but unfortunately for science, one of them was devoured by a cat and the other made its escape."[22] Despite this and several other accounts, no specimen was recorded, and it was not until 1979 that an unmarked specimen was found in the archives of the Muséum d'Histoire Naturelle in Marseille by the curator. Realizing the size of the specimen was significantly larger than the largest recorded gecko species, Alain Delcourt sent the specimen to the United States for study. Aaron Bauer and Tony Russell, specialists in gecko taxonomy, examined the specimen and found that it belonged in a group of geckos, the *Carphodactylini*, that occur only in New Zealand, New

Caledonia, and parts of Australia. Furthermore, they were certain that it was a species of *Hoplodactylus*, a genus known only from New Zealand. During a visit to New Zealand, Bauer uncovered Maori and colonialist accounts of tree-dwelling lizards.

Due to a loss of records at the Marseille museum, it is not possible to identify for certain where the specimen came from. Bauer and Russell published a paper in 1987 linking the specimen with accounts of the kawekaweau.[23] However, other researchers have noted the lack of subfossil records for a large lizard in New Zealand.[24] It is unlikely the specimen will ever be conclusively shown to be from New Zealand.

Is it possible that the specimen is the kawekaweau? Beyond that, is it possible that the legendary kawekaweau still lives high above the ground on the islands? There seems to be a scarcity of reports that would suggest that the creature survived past the nineteenth century, but, much like the discovery of the specimen, anything can happen.

Huia

The story of the huia is a sad tale. Sometimes called "the sacred bird," the huia was hunted by the Maori as a status symbol, prized for its plumage and skin as a decoration of rank in Maori culture. This marked the beginning of its decline, as its habitat was reduced by the hunting of it. However, this became much more pronounced with the arrival of Europeans.[25]

Noted for its distinctive sexual dimorphism, with females sporting an elongated, curved beak that the males lacked, the bird was hunted by Europeans to mount them in both private and museum collections. Deforestation also posed a major issue for the huia, as the bird depended on the rotting wood of primary forests to scavenge for insects.[26]

Colonialist and naturalist Sir Walter Buller recorded the bird in his seminal work *A history of the birds of New Zealand*, which is the most complete account of the bird and Maori traditions surrounding it.[27] Buller was notable for exporting the hunted birds while writing accounts of his hunts that are profoundly disturbing today:

> In a few seconds, without sound or warning of any kind, a huia came bounding along, almost tumbling, through the close foliage of the pukapuka, and presented himself to view at such close range that it was impossible to fire. This gave me an opportunity of watching this beautiful bird and marking his noble bearing, if I may so express it, before I shot him.[28]

The bird was declared extinct in 1907 despite attempts by Maori elders to have it protected legally.[29] Reports were recorded into the 1920s.[30] An expedition in the rural Akatarawa River valley was conducted in February 1924 by C. W. G. Betts, although this expedition could not find any trace of the bird.[31] The last recorded sighting of the bird occurs in the 1970s, although some still believe that the bird could be hiding out in the more rural areas of the North Island, although there is little to support these beliefs.

There is an effort to clone the animal from the ample museum specimens, although researchers note issues with the genetic diversity of a bird that was already rare by the time these specimens were collected.[32] These efforts might prove to be the only avenue for a return of the species.

Laughing Owl

The laughing owl of New Zealand is most notable for its namesake sound, described by those who heard it as a "loud cry made up of a series of dismal shrieks frequently repeated" and also compared to that of a young dog.[33] The bird was first described in 1845 by European colonizers, who found them in plentiful numbers.[34] However, by 1880, the population numbers of the bird species were rapidly declining, presumably due to the introduction of stoats, ferrets, and cats that both directly harmed individual owls and their primary prey, the Pacific rat. The last known specimen was found dead in 1914 in the middle of a road in Canterbury.[35]

Following the bird's extinction, reports continued throughout the century. The first of these was a report of a single bird calling at Wairaumoana, the southwestern arm of Lake Waikaremoana, in 1925.[36] Another report followed in 1927.[37] Naturalist Brian Parkinson reports in

The Travelling Naturalist that he heard laughing owl vocalizations in the 1940s.[38]

Hall-Jones reported from Saddle Hill of an unidentified bird emitting "a most unusual weird cry which might almost be described as maniacal" and postulated that the animal was the laughing owl. This report from 1956 seems to be the last sighting of the bird.[39] Williams and Harrison indicated that fragments of a laughing owl egg were found in 1960, indicating that a small population may have survived to that point.[40]

While the laughing owl may have surpassed its given year of extinction by several decades, there is little to say that the bird survived past the 1970s; although, on an island as large as New Zealand, anything is possible, even if unlikely. Naturalist Errol Fuller gave his opinion on the laughing owl as such:

> Anyone still believing in the laughing owl's survival and hoping to find its last resting place, might do worse than learn to play the accordion..."It could always be brought from its lurking place in the rocks, after dusk, by the strains of an accordion. Soon after the music had commenced the bird would silently flit over and face the performer, and finally take up its station in the vicinity, and remain within easy hearing till it had ceased."[41]

Greater short-tailed bat

Three species of bats are the endemic mammals of New Zealand. Of these, the greater short-tailed bat is presumed to be extinct, last sighted in 1967. The enigmatic bat disappeared from New Zealand's North and South Islands following European arrival in the 1640s. It was then restricted to small predator-free islands such as Big South Cape and the Solomon Islands until rats were accidentally introduced in 1963.[42] While several rare species of birds were evacuated, the greater short-tailed bat was not so fortunate.[43]

The International Union for Conservation of Nature's Red List lists the following information on the species, last updated in 2008:

Rats have been eradicated from both Big South Cape (where the species was last seen) and neighbouring Putauhina Island. Following these eradications, there have been several reports of bat sightings from Putauhina, and in 1999 Colin O'Donnell recorded *Mystacina*-like echolocation calls from the island that do not belong to *M. tuberculata*. There have also been two unconfirmed reports of bats being seen on Big South Cape. The identity of the bats being seen still must be confirmed, and although *M. tuberculata* is thought to have once inhabited these islands, the nearest populations of it or the only other New Zealand bat species (*Chalinolobus tuberculatus*) are more than 50 km away. For this reason, there is a real possibility that *M. robusta* still survives in low numbers.[44]

In addition to O'Donnell's 1999 expedition, an expedition in 2009 was unable to find any trace of the species.[45] It is unknown if any additional expeditions are being planned to find a trace of the bat species.

Moa

Moa were nine species of flightless birds endemic to New Zealand, closely related to the South American tinamous order and also commonly placed within the ratite group that also includes ostriches and emus. The two largest species of moa, *Dinornis robustus* and *Dinornis novaezelandiae*, stood at about 3.6 meters, while *Anomalopteryx parva* was not much larger than a turkey.[46] Their extinction occurred between 1300 and 1440, primarily due to overhunting by the Maori, who frequently made lavish meals of moas and their eggs.[47] Despite being believed to be extinct for possibly seven hundred years, reported sightings persist.

The earliest reports of survival appear to be from the late nineteenth century. Charles Gould writes in *Mythical Monsters* (1886):

I believe the Nestor is still, rarely, met with. Mr. [Gideon] Mantell is of the opinion that the Moa and his congeners continued in existence long after the advent of the aboriginal Maori. Mr. Mantell discovered a gigantic fossil egg, presumably that of the Moa.[48]

Atholl Anderson collects some European reports up to the end of the nineteenth century in the research paper "On Evidence For the Survival of Moa in European Fiordland," which focuses on the survival of one species in a particular area of New Zealand past the 1770s.[49]

Reports have continued in the twentieth and twenty-first centuries. A 1993 sighting by Paddy Freaney, a publican (hotel owner) from Arthur's Pass, was reported in the Craigieburn Range in Canterbury, resulting in the planning of an investigation by the Department of Conservation.[50] However, it was found that a photo taken by Freaney of the "moa" was a red deer, as identified by Dr. Richard Holdaway, a paleo-ecologist with the University of Canterbury.[51]

Bruce Spittle recorded 150 sightings in *Moa Sightings*, ranging from 1500 to throughout the nineteenth century, concluding with the Canterbury sighting/photograph.[52] Several expeditions have been mounted to find conclusive evidence that the moa survives, including one presented in a 2002 episode of *Animal X*, but none have found evidence.[53]

CHAPTER 10

PAPUA NEW GUINEA

Dobsegna

THE THYLACINE HAS BECOME a symbol of the woes of human-made extinctions and the potential for de-extinction, but many still believe that it lives on. While the existence of the creature on mainland Australia and Tasmania has been explored in this book previously, for now, we will look into this cryptid's so-called "cousin," the dobsegna, a similar creature reported in New Guinea.[1]

During the Pleistocene epoch, ending a mere 11,700 years ago, the thylacine was extant in New Guinea, as we know from the fossil record. According to reports from as late as the 1990s, creatures resembling the thylacine have been spotted in Irian Jaya, New Guinea's less-explored western, Indonesian half.[2] According to George M. Eberhart, the creatures are described as having "Light-brown fur. Strong mouth. Huge jaws. Head and shoulders like a dog. Stripes on the rear portion of its body. Thin tail nearly as long as its body."[3] The description highly resembles that of the Tasmanian tiger.

Several locations, in particular, have experienced many sightings, such as Gunsung Lorentz National Park and Mount Giluwe.[4] In 1993, cattle farmer Ned Terry, inspired by such reports, traveled to visit the local Dai people and showed them images of thylacines, which they identified as the dobsegna.[5] While the last sighting seems to have occurred in 1997, the vast jungles of New Guinea do provide massive amounts of cover for a potential animal to hide in, making this an interesting case.[6]

Gazeka

In 1875, the eminent English scientific journal *Nature* carried several letters from Alfred O. Walker concerning the recent discovery by Lieutenant Sidney Smith and Captain Moresby from HMS *Basilisk* of a startlingly large heap of fresh dung in a forest while surveying Papua New Guinea's north coast, between Huon Bay and Cape Basilisk. The pile of excrement was so big and its overall appearance was such that the men assumed it to have been left by some form of rhinoceros; however, as noted by the editor of *Nature*, no species of rhinoceros is known to exist on Papua New Guinea.[7] The German naturalist and zoologist Adolf Bernhard Meyer published a response in *Nature*, in which he mentions this possible existence of an unidentified creature, writing:

I agree with you that the presence of Rhinoceros in New Guinea must be seriously questioned, but I would like to mention a description of a very large quadruped in New Guinea, that I obtained from the Papuans of the south coast of Geelvinks Bay. (...) While I was hunting wild pigs with the Papuans, they told me, before I asked, [of] a very large pig, as they called it, fixing its height on a tree trunk over [1.80 meters]. I could not obtain other information from them, except that the beast was very rare, but they were very accurate in their assertion. I promised lots of beads and knives to the man who would bring me something [sic] this big animal, but none did.[8]

This description of a pig-creature, sometimes said to resemble a tapir, is referred to as the Gazeka or the Papuan Devil-Pig. Local indigenous people describe the creature as having a long, proboscis-like snout, and therefore it was believed by the explorers to resemble a tapir or giant sloth.[9]

Karl Shuker records an alleged encounter with these creatures on an expedition by Australian explorer Captain Charles A. W. Monckton:

On May 10, two of his team's members, an army private called Ogi and a village constable called Oina, were sent on ahead to investigate a track discovered by the expedition the previous day. Somehow the two men became separated, and while seeking Oina, Ogi came upon two extraordinary creatures grazing nearby.

CAROL SCOTT

Although vaguely pig-like, each of these animals was approximately 3.5 ft tall, and 5 ft long, with a very dark, patterned hide, cloven feet, a long snout, and a horse-like (hairy?) tail. Ogi was so frightened by these weird creatures, which he referred to as devil-pigs as he felt sure that they must be demons in porcine guise, that he tried to shoot one, but missed. What happened after that is unclear, because when he was later found by Oina and taken back to camp, Ogi was in a severe state of shock, and unable to recollect anything further.[10]

In 1987, mammalogist James I. Menzies proposed a dramatic identity for the gazeka. He claimed that the beast was a *palorchestid diprotodon* – a large and very bizarre-looking herbivorous marsupial, which did indeed have big eyes, a short trunk, well-delineated external ears and would have resembled a tapir or a pig. Such creatures are found in the fossil record in Australia up to thirteen thousand years ago.[11] Cryptozoologist Bernard Heuvelmans also endorsed this theory.[12] Another proposed explanation recorded by Karl Shuker is the *Palorchestes*, a herbivorous marsupial, also from Australia, that went extinct eleven thousand years ago.[13]

Ropen

The ropen, a bat-like creature, hails from Papua New Guinea. The creature reportedly has a long tail with a delta-shaped tip and a beak filled with needle-sharp teeth.[14] In addition, the creature is said to have a four-to-six-foot wingspan.[15] Reports have also surfaced on the creature being bioluminescent.[16] Sightings of the creature began as early as the 1940s when Christian missionaries came to the island; researcher Nick Redfern notes a decline in reports in recent years.[17]

The creature has become an object of fascination for Young Earth Creationists, those who believe that the Earth is much younger than what mainstream scientists propose; as such, creationists believe that a living dinosaur would prove their theory of the Earth's timeline.[18] Cryptozoologists, such as Nick Redfern, have proposed that reports of a creature in Papua New Guinea are that of a living pterodactyl, although Redfern notes that the creatures reported are much smaller than the historical creature.

In 2006, a Texan named Paul Nation traveled to Papua New Guinea's interior and set up camp in a local village near a rumored ropen roost. He never saw the creatures directly but captured footage of their "lights" in the sky. After a few nights of observation, Nation left his post with no evidence of the creature.[19] However, in his breakdown of major "living pterodactyl" reports, scientist Glen J. Kuban notes several confounding factors in these reports. He notes that "ropen" means "bird" in many areas of Papua New Guinea, as well as writing that:

> ...the Ropen legends are multifaceted, and to the extent real creatures may be involved, they may involve more than one kind of animal (with living pterosaurs the least likely). For reasons explained earlier, it's likely that at

least some sightings of alleged pterosaurs in PNG are misidentified large birds. There are [sic] no shortage of possible candidates, since over 800 species of birds have been documented in PNG, with over a dozen being herons and egrets, besides frigate birds, eagles, storks, cranes, pelicans, hornbills, and others with large wingspans, some of which are also crested. Other "Ropen" sightings may be explained by fruit bats. Some fruit bats such as "flying foxes" grow quite large (with wingspans over 4 feet across), and if seen in silhouette (which would be the case at night) can present a pterosaur-like profile, especially to nonscientific observers.[20]

CHAPTER 11

PHILIPPINES

Amomongo

IN THE SUMMER OF 2008, reports came from the Philippines of a man-sized ape creature with nails of incredible length. The creature reportedly attacked two residents and killed farm animals in the area, eating their entrails.[1] Police in La Castellana confirmed that one of the men was treated for scratches on different parts of his body.[2] Described as around five feet tall, the amomongo of the 2008 attacks is said to be incredibly violent. Some reports have stated the creature lives in caves near the active volcano Mount Kanlaon.[3]

The term *amomongo* is derived from the Hiligaynon word *amó*, which means "ape" or "monkey." Traditional Filipino folklore tells of an amomongo who is challenged by a firefly he previously berated and is subsequently defeated in a fight between them.[4] The amomongo is characterized as an angry, even vengeful creature, although the moral of the story teaches that even the smallest creatures can defeat their foes.

Reports of the creature ceased after the 2008 attacks in Negros Occidental, prompting some to argue that it was simply a case of shared psychosis among residents. The short span of the attacks may also indicate that the attacks were the result of an angered, territorial, or rabid crab-eating macaque or another primate. Mayor Alberto Nicor said the amomongo is not a witch but a wild animal and added the animal may have been suffering from hunger.[5]

Kapre

The kapre is a creature shrouded in folk mythology, with a significant number of local legends about its actions and habits. Some historians believe that the term was spread by the Spanish colonizers of the Philippines to dissuade Filipinos from aiding escaped slaves. The term is derived from the Arabic *kafir* (referring to a nonbeliever in the Islamic faith) and the creature is often said to carry a large cigar. The similarly dark colour of escaped slaves and the kapre, as well as the association with cigars, lends credence to the idea that the idea was propagated by the Spanish.[6] Some reports have the kapre wearing a traditional loincloth known as *bahag*.

In pre-colonization Philippines, animist beliefs stated that a huge black spirit watched people from the trees.[7] Later characterizations of the kapre state that they dwell in big trees, such as bamboo, mango, acacia, and banyan.

The kapre is often characterized as a prankster in stories lacking the more mythical elements.[8] Such pranks might include rustling tree branches to scare people, laughing loudly at night, creating smoke in the trees, as well as appearing before people to scare them.[9] These reports share similarities with reports from North America about the Sasquatch, which also frequently rustles trees and makes calls at night.

More mythical elements of the kapre legend include the idea that it wears a belt that can be used to make itself invisible to humans, possesses a white stone that can grant wishes, and can follow people it "befriends," invisible to the rest of society.

As can be seen from the heavy mythological influence, it is unlikely that the kapre is based on an existing animal, although some reports may be conflated with other Filipino crypto-primates.

Sigbin

A creature of Philippino mythology, the sigbin is said to be a shape-shifting, bloodsucking creature. Due to its alleged ability to shape-shift, the creature has been described in various forms, with the most common characterization being a doglike creature with long back legs similar to that of a kangaroo.[10] The creature is often associated with the aswang in mythology, serving as a pet that can bite victims on the neck and draw their blood.[11] Fantastical elements of sigbin mythology include the ability to turn invisible, shape-shift, clap using its ears, and use its tail as a whip.[12]

The creature resembles North American reports of the chupacabra, which is also said to be a bloodsucking animal with many forms. Jennifer Rivkin notes that both creatures also have a penchant for emitting a foul smell.[13] In 2003, researchers on a World Wildlife Fund expedition in Borneo first described the cat-fox, a mysterious carnivore that superficially resembles reports of the sigbin based upon its physiology.[14] However, there is no conclusive link between reports of the sigbin and the cat-fox.

CHAPTER 12

RUSSIA

Abnauayu

MUCH LIKE THE previously discussed Almas, the Abnauayu are reported wildmen of the Caucasus Mountains region.[1] The Abkhazians, an ethnic group that resides in Abkhazia, a disputed region on the northeastern coast of the Black Sea, have reported a humanoid figure for centuries.[2] The general description is similar to other tall hairy humanoids, with reddish-black hair, low forehead, and muscular arms and legs.[3]

The creature is most well-known from the Zana of Abkhazia controversy. As Margaryan et al. describes in the paper "The genomic origin of Zana of Abkhazia":

> The local folklore of the South Caucasus region of Abkhazia records a "wild woman" named Zana, who lived in the 19th century, who was referred to by some locals as a female Abnauayu or Almasty...Originally

captured while living outdoors in the forest, Zana was later enslaved by a succession of local wealthy individuals, and was finally bought by the Abkhaz nobleman Edgi Genaba who took her to his estate at Tkhina, where she lived until her death around 1890.

Inspired by the speculation that she might have been a female Yeti, Soviet scientists visited the region in 1962 to gather descriptions and accounts from the elders living in the village of Tkhina, who still recalled her. The locals described her as being "part human and part animal," 2 m tall and dark-skinned, covered with thick hair, who was able to lift a 50 kg sack of flour with one hand, and outrun a horse in a race. According to the eyewitness accounts she also lacked speech, which along with her alleged strange behavior and appearance, likely resulted in her reputation as an Almasty. Zana is also documented to have given birth to two sons and two daughters from local men. Following her death, she was buried in the Genabas' family cemetery, and although the exact location of Zana's burial site was unknown, the grave of her youngest son, Khwit, was identified in 1971. After several attempts to locate Zana's burial site, the remains of an anonymous female were discovered in the Genabas' family cemetery, leading to speculation that they may have belonged to Zana herself[4]

The report sequenced the DNA of the unknown female and Zana's son and concluded that the unknown female was Zana. Additionally, they were also to conclude that she was a human woman of east African descent with unique physical characteristics. By this account, Zana was simply a human woman who was forced into slavery for having unusual physical characteristics.

Brosno dragon

The Brosno dragon (also referred to Brosny or Brosnya) is an alleged lake monster in Russia's Lake Brosno, which is about 43 meters (140 feet) at its deepest point. Located in western Russia, Lake Brosno is near Andreapol and approximately 443 kilometers from Moscow. The Brosno dragon is reportedly sixteen feet long and is covered in iridescent scales that glow due to their bioluminescence.[5]

One of the first stories in which the Brosno dragon appears dates back to the thirteenth century. According to the legend, the Tatar-Mongol army encountered the creature while traveling to the city of Novgorod during the Mongol invasion of Kievan Rus:

> The group's leader and the grandson of Genghis Khan, Batu Khan, decided to stop at Lake Brosno so his men and their horses could rest. As the horses approached the water to drink, an enormous creature sprang out of the lake and surprised the horses and men. Although the terrified army tried to run, Brosny opened its huge mouth and devoured many of the men and their horses. Those lucky enough to survive fled. The terrible event horrified them so greatly that the survivors decided to end their journey.[6]

I could not find the original source for this particular story, although it is true that the Mongols never conquered Novgorod.

Vikings are another group who reportedly encountered the creature in the thirteenth century. Another piece of folklore states that the Brosno dragon swallowed a Nazi pilot and his plane whole when it either crashed or flew low to the lake.[7]

A photograph of the creature was taken in 1997; however, the photo seems to be lost now.

Various explanations have been suggested for the Brosno dragon, including misidentification of pike, an underwater volcano causing wakes, and general superstition or hoaxes. Tver region paleontologist Nikolai Dikov was quoted as saying that based upon the photographs, this creature was probably related to an animal of decidedly prehistoric origin:

> The creature's alleged shape suggested an extinct order of reptiles with teeth like mammals. The "extinct order of reptiles" that Dikov was referring to is probably of the family known as Synapsids, whose teeth were differentiated into molars, canines, and incisors, similar to mammals' teeth.[8]

CHAPTER 13

SINGAPORE

Bukit Timah Monkey Man

THE BUKIT TIMAH Monkey Man is "Singapore's Bigfoot." Singapore is an island-city state in Southeast Asia with a high population density; however, the Bukit Timah area of the city has forested regions in which a supposed hominid is said to reside. First reported in the 1800s, a time of major development for the island, reports have continued up to 2020, often sporadically.

The first report came in 1805 from a Malay elder, who reported seeing an "upright monkey, one with somewhat human characteristics."[1] In his work *The Bigfoot Book*, Nick Redfern records the following from sixty-five-year-old Bukit Panjang:

> We were always told as children when in the Kampung not to go near the forest at night due to the Monkey Man. Of course, we never saw it ourselves but it was

always some uncle or friend of the family [who] had seen it.[2]

Japanese soldiers reported seeing the creature during the era of Japanese occupation, although I could not find exact details on these reports.[3]

Some reports from locals have emerged in the twenty-first century. According to one unnamed taxi driver:

When driving my taxi past the fire station on Upper Bukit Timah Road in the middle of the night I hit what I thought was a child that ran out in the middle of the road. It was on the car bonnet and then snarled at me – it was like a monkey but so big! It ran off injured covered in blood, and holding its arm which was broken.[4]

Another report, from another unnamed local:

I was going to the bus stop early one morning to catch the bus 171. It was very foggy and cold. I thought I saw a tramp going through the rubbish bin, however when I approached, it called out with a loud animal sound and ran back into the forest. It was grey, hairy and ran on two legs, but had a monkey's face. I was shivering with fear and called the police but to no avail.[5]

Bukit Timah rainforest has a fairly small area of 1.6 square kilometers and is surrounded by residential development. For this reason, it would be difficult for a large primate to survive in this area with so few eyewitness reports. Skeptics argue that people could be mistaking the crab-eating macaque, a species of monkey common to that area, for a large primate.

CHAPTER 14

SRI LANKA

Nittaewo

AN INTERESTING CASE of crypto-anthropology is the Nittaewo, an alleged tribe of ape-like humanoids in Sri Lanka that were supposedly driven to extinction by a genocide by the Vedda, one of the indigenous tribes on the island. No archaeological evidence has been found for the tribe, and all evidence comes from accounts recorded in the late nineteenth century and early twentieth century from Vedda elders.

According to tradition, the Nittaewo were a diminutive people that stood at about three to four feet tall, were bipedal, and were "extremely primitive." In some accounts, their humanlike bodies were covered with reddish fur. The Nittaewo were said to sleep in caves and crevices and "surrounded their prey, jumping in and ripping it open with their long nails."[1] Reports from Vedda elders stated that the two groups were constant enemies until the Veddas of Lenama rounded up the Nittaewo into a cave, placed burning bushwood at the entrance, and allowed the Nittaewo to suffocate.[2] Bernard Heuvelmans estimates that the genocide likely took place around 1800.

Ctesias, a Greek physician in the Persian court during the fourth century BC, wrote about "little people" with nails "like those of an animal" inhabiting Sri Lanka, then referred to as "Taprobane."[3] Pliny the Elder also reported "half men and half beasts" lived on Ceylon, another ancient name for Sri Lanka.[4] In 1886, Hugh Nevill wrote the article "The Nittaewo of Ceylon," giving a tale as such:

> The Nittaewo were a cruel and savage race of men, rather dark, living in small communities at Lenama. They built platforms in trees, covered with a thatch of leaves, and in these they lived. They could neither speak Vedda, Sinhalese or Tamil, but their language sounded like the Telegu of pilgrims to Kattragam. They attacked anything including Veddas and no Vedda dare enter their district to hunt or collect honey. Many years ago the ancestors of the informants fought with these Nittaewo, and finally, drove the remnant of them into a cavern. Before this they piled firewood and kept up the fire for three days, after which the race became extinct, and their district a favourite hunting ground of these Veddas.[5]

The Veddas of Lenama went extinct just a few generations after the alleged genocide of the Nittaewo. Thus, the location of the cave where the genocide occurred has been lost, and all knowledge of the Nittaewo come from third-hand accounts, as Nevill and other researchers of the era received information from other Veddas groups.

Ven. Thambugala Anandasiri, a monk residing in the area, recorded an account of the genocide allegedly passed down through generations.

The Veddas had a discussion and organized themselves to eradicate the Nittaewo menace once and for all. Armed with bows and arrows, the Veddas hid in the area frequented by the Nittaewo. Two of the Veddas were sent to a flat rock used as a resting place (Wadigala). As the Nittaewo never faced the Veddas in an open fight but used to ambush them, the task of the two decoys was to find the gathering place of the Nittaewo. In the evening, [a] few Nittaewo approached the resting Veddas. After having a good look at the Veddas, the Nittaewo went back intending to return in the night to kill them for meat. However, unknown to the Nittaewo, the two Veddas followed them to their lair and in the early morning led the rest of the Veddas there. Then followed a massacre of the Nittaewo, who tried their best to retaliate, but were no match for the arrows of the Veddas. Six of the Nittaewo who were the sole survivors of the battle that raged the whole day, managed to hide in a cave situated on the south slope of Kutumbiyagala (now Kudumbigala). The Veddas who came in pursuit surrounded the cave and burned the Nittaewo to death. Two of the Nittaewo managed to escape and lived for a while in a hill at Okanda. They too, were subsequently killed by the Villagers. After exterminating the Nittaewo, the Veddas occupied Lenama.[6]

Fredrick Lewis, a businessman who served as the Assistant Conservator of Forests in Sri Lanka, wrote in his work "Notes on an exploration in Eastern Uva and Southern Panama Pattu" that he had met a man whose grandfather had participated in the genocide of the Nittaewo.[7]

In 1945, British primatologist W. C. Osman Hill led an expedition to the island and found that belief in the Nittaewo was widespread amongst the Vedda population.[8]

Allegedly, a Spanish anthropologist by the name of Dr. Salvador Martinez spotted a Nittaewo in 1984.[9] However, I could not find the original source of the claim and could not locate an anthropologist by that name. Of course, that does not necessarily mean that the sighting did not occur. However, a sighting of a Nittaewo over 150 years after the alleged genocide would be a twist to an already obscure mystery.

A variety of explanations have been presented to explain the Nittaewo mystery. In his excellent work on the mystery, Pradeep A. Jayatunga identifies key theories and explores the possibility of each. Such theories include the Nittaewo being an outcast tribe or a group of feral humans, a remnant population of early man (such as surviving

Neanderthals or, more likely, *Homo florensis*), an unknown population of Negrito people, and confusion with local and possibly now-extinct populations of monkey or bear. In fact, Jayatunga found in reviewing Neville's writings that the Nittaewo may be a case of two pieces of folklore being conflated. Quoting Neville:

> At the account of their shaggy red hair and long claws, the Veddas were much amused. They at once said the Sinhalese were confusing with the Nittaewo the rare sun-bear, or Rahu walas, now extinct at Lenama, and unknown to the Sinhalese, except by gossip.[10]

Jayatunga analyzes the idea that some of the characteristics of the Nittaewo came from a possibly extinct brown bear in the area:

> But what if there were two different rare/extinct creatures with their own separate legends? The passage of time, confusion, ignorance and the human penchant for the sensational would have combined the two in a tale of mysterious half-man, half-ape/bear type of beings. In fact, that is exactly what the Veddas who were amused by the confusion of the two legends explained to Neville! Instances of two or more separate legends, over time, being amalgamated into one are not rare in folklore.

There had been evidence of a species red/brown bear in the area. In addition to the existence of the remains studied by Pucheran at the Museum of Natural History in Paris, Henry Parker and Neville state that the sightings of this bear had been reported from Padawiya and the eastern province respectively. More recently, in the Administrative Report of the Warden, Dept. of Wildlife, for 1952, C. W. Nicholas says that the existence of a brown bear in the northern part of Yala Strict Natural reserve "is still believed in and there are men who claim to have seen it in recent years."

This animal is described as being more gregarious, aggressive, and fierce than the sloth bear though smaller in size. It makes a good candidate for the identity of the shaggy red haired creature with long claws feared by the Veddas in the legend.

The villagers who had no firsthand experience of either of the two creatures could easily have confused the descriptions of the fierce, rare brown bear with the Veddas' tales of the savage Nittaewo tribe. Both were enemies of and feared by the Veddas. It is clear that at the time of Neville's investigations, the Veddas (at least some of them) were well aware of the two different legends. However, even by that time, the villagers in their confusion had thoroughly mixed the two up. It is likely that the legend of the extinct Nittaewo, being the more mysterious (and therefore more interesting and wider/faster spreading), acquired the red hair and bear-like claws from the tale of the rare animal.

In any event, it is a natural human tendency to attribute animal characteristics to savage or less civilized people. The primitive aggressive and isolated human tribe, who were dreaded enemies of the Veddas and as a result were exterminated, would have acquired, in the legend among the villagers, the characteristics of a fierce animal (seldom seen even by the Veddas) which too, in its turn became extinct and gained legendary status. Even during Neville's time, there may have been only a handful of Veddas who were capable of explaining the confusion of the two tales and the resultant posthumous appellation of the "hairy beasts with claws" tag to the Nittaewos. Both the originating creatures being extinct, the amalgamated legends remained unravelled and quite possibly acquired more combined animal/human hybrid details.[11]

Whatever the case, the Nittaewo present an interesting case of the intersection of cultural facts and folklore. Further investigations into Vedda legends and anthropology expeditions to this area of Sri Lanka may be needed to settle this mystery.

It is worth noting that Neville's writings have not been very preserved. The original copies are in very poor condition and few scans exist.[12] Researchers wishing to preserve the culture of the Veddas and the work of Neville are needed to protect this important information from being lost.

Devil Bird

The devil bird is a creature from Sri Lankan mythology. Its most distinctive feature is that it emits a "bloodcurdling" human-sounding shriek at night.[13] The shriek of the bird, also called the *ulama*, is said to foretell death, much like the banshee of Irish mythology. One Mr Fitford, of the Ceylon Civil Service, compared the sound to "a boy in torture, whose screams are being stopped by being strangled."[14]

Writer Ria Rameez gives the origins of the devil bird in folklore as such:

> The stories surrounding Sri Lanka's devil bird are just as terrifying as the cry itself. In one of them, a man who suspected his wife of infidelity murdered their infant son in her absence, and when she arrived, served her with a curry prepared with the child's flesh. Not suspecting anything, the woman ate the gruesome meal, until she unearthed a finger of her beloved child. Frenzied with grief and horror, she fled screaming into the forest, where she was transformed into the ulama. As the tale goes, her anguished wails and screams still echo through the forest, terrifying villagers and bringing doom to all those who hear it.[15]

The identity of the bird is still up for debate, although the legend is generally considered to be an exaggeration of the very real spot-bellied eagle-owl (*Bubo nipalensis*) by ornithologists.[16] Other possible identities include the forest eagle-owl (*Bubo nipalensis*), the crested honey-buzzard

(*Pernis ptilorhynchus ruficollis*), and various eagles.[17] As the bird is not usually seen and its cry only described in vague terms, the devil bird reports might also refer to the Ceylon highland nightjar (*Caprimulgus indicus kelaarti*), which is small and not particularly frightening, as an owl's deflective eyes may be at night.

CHAPTER 15
TURKEY

Lake Van Monster

IN 2017, an interesting find was discovered in the depths of Lake Van, which is the second largest lake in Turkey.[1] Divers searching for a lake monster instead found a three-thousand-year-old, mile-wide castle at the bottom of the lake, a relict of a Bronze Age empire. That's not the only secret the lake has hidden: in 2016, the team also discovered a two-square-mile field of stalagmites known as "underwater fairy chimneys." They also found one-thousand-year-old gravestones and, in January, a sunken Russian ship believed to have gone down in 1948.[2]

But could the lake be hiding a living lake monster?

The first alleged encounter with the Lake Van Monster occurred in 1889, wherein a man was dragged into the lake despite the efforts of his companions. This was allegedly published in the April 29, 1889, edition of the Ottoman newspaper *Saadet,* but I was unable to verify this.

Other sources say that the first sighting occurred in 1995, leading to a rash of over a thousand sightings.[3] An alleged video of the creature was recorded in 1997 by local teaching assistant Unal Kozak, who had previously published a book on the creature. The short video shows something rising from the lake, moving to the left, and then submerging once again.[4]

The creature is described as "long and dark" and "looks like a dinosaur."[5] While the living plesiosaurus theory is popular, some cryptozoologists make the interesting deduction based on the Kozak video that the creature could be a squid of some sort, based on the movement of the creature in the video.[6] However, it is worth noting that the video has been criticized due to its low quality and the allegation that it is a latex dummy being dragged behind a boat, which is out of frame. The general consensus is that the sightings were a hoax to drive tourism to the town.[7]

CHAPTER 16

VIETNAM

Batutut

ON THE NORTH Central Coast of Vietnam lies Vũ Quang, an inhospitable area that presented some of the greatest biological discoveries of the 1990s after an expedition discovered several new varieties of deer and antelope. The rainy season frequently leads to days of precipitation, while the dry season presents a constant fog. Local hunters often avoid the area, set traps, or release trained dogs rather than hunting themselves. The Vietnamese revolutionary Phan Đình Phùng used the area as a headquarters while fighting the colonial French Empire, using the hidden location to lead the revolutionary forces to victory.[1]

A variety of different sources have reported seeing a hairy manlike creature known as the batutut in the densely wooded areas of Vietnam and its island neighbor Borneo, including Vietnamese locals, French explorers, and American scholars. Dr. John MacKinnon of the World Wildlife

Fund, who went on to discover the saola, wrote the 1975 book *In Search Of The Red Ape*, which includes a section on his discovery of prints from an unknown primate:

> The rhino may be rare but at least it is a well-known and scientifically documented animal, which is more than can be said of Batutut. I was travelling alone along a hill ridge on the far side of the river where I had never ventured before. The path was good, though rather muddy, and I hadn't a care in the world. Suddenly I stopped dead, amazed at what I saw. I knelt down to examine the disturbing footprint in the earth, a print so like a man's yet so definitely not a man's that my skin crept and I felt a strong desire to head home. The print was roughly triangular in shape, about six inches long by four across. The toes looked quite human, as did the shapely heel, but the sole was both too short and too broad to be that of a man and the big toe was on the opposite side to what seemed to be the arch of the foot.
>
> Back at camp I showed him my sketches and asked what animal could make such tracks. Without a moment's hesitation he replied "Batutut" but when I asked him to describe the beast he said it was not an animal but a type of ghost. Bahat gave an imitation of its plaintive call, a drawn-out tootootootootoo, from which it derives its name, and told me many stories about this shy, nocturnal creature, who lives deep in the jungle feeding on river snails, which it breaks open with stones. Batutut, he told me, is about four feet tall,

walks upright like a man and has a long black mane. It is said to be fond of children, whom it lures away from their villages but does them no harm. To adults, however, it never shows itself, but occasionally men had been found that Batutut had killed and ripped open to feast on their liver (to Malays the seat of all emotions, analogous to the European heart). Like the other spirits of the forest the creature is very shy of light and fire. Bahat said that, as a young boy, he, too, had seen the footprints of Batutut and other villagers had also seen them from time to time.[2]

A North Vietnamese general ordered an expedition to find the creature in 1974, which was unsuccessful in finding any trace of the creature.[3]

The creature is described as being approximately 1.8 meters (5.9 feet) and bipedal with a variety of colorizations, including black, brown, and gray. Reports also state that the batutut has "a noticeable, thick mane of hair that runs down the back of its head, not unlike that of a horse."[4] There are differing reports on the creature being both solitary and being seen in groups, indicating that the creature could vary its grouping habits.

Several casts have been made in addition to the tracks found by MacKinnon. A set of footprints was found in 1982 by Professor Tran Hong Viet of the Pedagogic University of Hanoi, measuring 28 by 16 centimeters (10 by 6.2 inches).[5] A picture of the prints was printed in the magazine *Fortean News of the World*.[6] An expedition by the television program *Destination Truth* for the fifth season premiere investigated a cast owned by a local primatologist. A cast made by the group later in the expedition was examined by Idaho State researcher Jeff Meldrum and declared to be "a significant discovery." However, like with the other casts, little came of the discovery.

Reports from nearby Borneo of the same, or a similar, creature state that the creature is extremely violent and willing to tear out the liver of humans. However, no reports have been recorded in the modern era.[7]

Dr. MacKinnon writes in *In Search of the Red Ape* that the alleged primate could be similar to the extinct humanoid *Meganthropus*. Noted cryptozoologist Loren Coleman has proposed that the creature could be a remnant population of *Homo erectus*.[8] Like many other alleged primates, some researchers have suggested misidentification of other humans or local primates.

Kting voar

The Kting voar ("wild cow with vine-like horns") is an alleged species of cow said to reside in Vietnam and Cambodia.[9] The species has the scientific nomenclature of *Pseudonovibos spiralis*, but it is debatable whether the species exists. The bovid received recognition through its distinctive horns, which are spiral and about forty-five centimeters (twenty inches) long. A set of horns was found by researchers in 1994 in a market in Ho Chi Minh City.[10]

The Kting voar is often associated with snakes and is

also known as the "snake-eating cow," which would be an unusual feature for a cow. However, a cow was photographed eating a snake in Australia in 2020, so it is possible that this is a rare behaviour that could occur in a bovid species.[11] However, research on bovids and snakes has not been conducted.

The Kting voar is only known through its distinctive horns; however, some specimens have been found to be domesticated cattle horns reshaped as a tourist attraction or anti-snake talisman.[12] Scientific debate on the existence of this alleged species peaked in the early 2000s, and efforts to conclusively find the creature do not seem to have been undertaken by mainstream scientists or cryptozoologists.

AFTERWORD

Our understanding of the natural world has long resulted in myths and legends. The legend of the cyclops, for example, was likely derived from the Greeks finding the fossils of the dwarf elephants on the island of Crete. Even many scientifically accepted species, such as the mountain gorilla, Komodo dragon, and the okapi, started off being dismissed as legends told by Indigenous populations around their habitats. It's quite possible that some of the animals in this book, many of them drawing from local folklore, could turn out to be incredibly real, providing credibility to cryptozoology and adding to our understanding of the natural world.

The best thing we can do is keep an open mind – not a gullible mind, but one open to facts and logic, to the stories of local populations that have existed for decades, if not centuries in many cases. Cryptozoology as a field should move in this direction with improved scientific understanding and data collection, constantly improving despite dismissal and ridicule.

That's how undiscovered creatures in the Asian and Oceania regions and beyond will be uncovered and protected, so that future scientists may gain a greater understanding of our natural world.

NOTES

INTRODUCTION

1. Hanneke Meijer. "Here Be Dragons: The Million-Year Journey of the Komodo Dragon." *The Guardian* (Guardian News & Media Limited, May 17, 2017). https://www.theguardian.com/science/2017/may/17/here-be-dragons-the-million-year-journey-of-the-komodo-dragon.
2. 2. David J. Daegling. *Bigfoot Exposed: An Anthropologist Examines America's Enduring Legend* (Lanham, MD: AltaMira Press, 2004).
3. "Data." North American Wood Ape Conservancy. Accessed 2022. https://reports.woodape.org/data/.
4. Bernard Heuvelmans. *On The Track of Unknown Animals* (Cambridge, MA: MIT Press, 1972).

1. AUSTRALIA

1. Joan Hughes, ed. *Australian Words and Their Origins* (Oxford, England: Oxford University Press, 1989).
2. George French Angus. *Savage Life and Scenes in Australia and New Zealand* (London, England: Smith, Elder, and Co, 1847).
3. Jonathan Maberry and David F. Kramer. *The Cryptopedia* (New York, NY: Kensington Publishing Corporation, 2007).
4. Robert Holden. *Bunyips: Australia's folklore of fear* (Canberra, Australia: National Library of Australia, 2001).
5. Pat Vikers-Rich, J.M. Monaghan, R.F. Baird, and T.H. Rich. *Vertebrate Palaeontology of Australasia* (Victoria, Australia: Pioneer Design Studio and Monash University, 1991).
6. Charles Fenner. *Bunyips and Billabongs* (Sydney, Australia: Angus and Robertson, 1933).
7. Tyler Houck. "The Burrunjor – A Present-Day Australian Dinosaur?" Tyler's Cryptozoo (blog), 2016).

8. Rex Gilroy. "'The Temple of Nim' Newsletter – 2006" (Mysterious Australia (blog), Katoomba, 2006).

9. Ralph E. Molnar. *Dragons in the dust: the paleobiology of the giant monitor lizard Megalania* (Bloomington, Alabama: Indiana University Press, 2004).

10. Bryan G. Fry, Stephen Wroe, Wouter Teeuwisse, et. al. "A central role for venom in predation by *Varanus komodoensis* (Komodo Dragon) and the extinct giant *Varanus* (*Megalania*) *priscus*" (Proceedings of the National Academy of Sciences of the United States of America 106, issue 22, Washington, DC, 2009).

11. Ralph E. Molnar. "History of monitors and their king" in Ruth Allen King, Eric R. Pianka, and Dennis King (eds.), *Varanoid lizards of the world* (Bloomington, Indiana: Indiana University Press, 2004).

12. See Note 14.

13. Jonathan Maberry and David F. Kramer. *The Cryptopedia* (New York, NY: Kensington Publishing Corp., 2007).

14. "The Extinction of Australian Megafauna" (*Convict Creations* (blog)).

15. Catalina Pimiento, Bruce J. MacFadden, Christopher F. Clements, et al. "Geographical distribution patterns of Carcharocles megalodon over time reveal clues about extinction mechanisms" (*Journal of Biogeography* 43, issue 8, 2016).

16. B.S. Roesch. "A Critical Evaluation of the Supposed Contemporary Existence of Carcharocles megalodon" (*The Cryptozoology Review* 3, issue 2, 1998).

17. J. Flanagin. "Sorry, Fans. Discovery Has Jumped the Shark Week" (*The New York Times*, 2014).

18. R. Aidan Martin. "Does Megalodon Still Live?" (ReefQuest Centre for Shark Research, n.d.).

19. Jonathan Maberry and David F. Kramer. *The Cryptopedia* (New York, NY: Kensington Publishing Corp., 2007).

20. Annie Potts, Philip Armstrong, and Deidre Brown. *A New Zealand Book of Beasts* (Auckland: Australia: Auckland University Press, 2013).

21. Carl Lumholtz, *Among Cannibals: An Account of Four Years' Travels in Australia and of Camp Life with the Aborigines of Queensland* (Cambridge, England: Cambridge University Press, 2010).

22. Brian Parkinson. *The Travelling Naturalist Around New Zealand* (London, England: Century Hutchinson, 1989).

23. Shuker, Karl. *In Search of Prehistoric Survivors* (London, England: Blandford Press, 1995).

24. See Note 27.

25. Errol Fuller. *Lost Animals: Extinction and the Photographic Record* (London, England: Bloomsbury Publishing, 2013).

26. See Note 27.

27. See Note 27.

28. See Note 27.

29. Ellis Troughton and Neville William Cayley. *Furred Animals of Australia* (Sydney, Australia: Angus & Robertson, 1973).

30. See Note 27.

31. See Note 27.

32. A.A. Burbidge and J. Woinarski. *"Thylacinus cynocephalus"* (The IUCN Red List of Threatened Species, Cambridge, 2016).

33. Rosemary Fleay-Thompson. "Expedition and Searches – 1937 to Present-Day" (NaturalWorlds, 2002).

34. Andy Park. "Tasmanian tiger – extinct or merely elusive?" (*Australian Geographic* 1, issue 3, Sydney, 1986).

35. Tasmania Parks and Wildlife Service. "Thylacine" (2013), quoted in Nick Redfern, *Monster Files* (Pompton Plains, New Jersey: New Page Books, 2013).

36. Nick Redfern. *Monster Files* (Pompton Plains, New Jersey: New Page Books, 2013).

37. "Thylacine Sighting Reports – 1 September 2016 to 19 September 2019" (Department of Primary Industries, Parks, Water and Environment, 2019).

38. "Superstitions of the Australian Aborigines: The Yahoo" (*Australian and New Zealand Monthly Magazine* 1, issue 2, 1842).

39. William Telfer. *The Wallabadah manuscript: recollections of the early days: the early history of the northern districts of New South Wales* (Sydney, Australia: New South Wales University Press, 1980).

40. Timothy Bull. *The Adventures of Tim the Yowie Man, cryptonaturalist* (Melbourne, Australia: Random House Australia, 2001).

41. Matt Cunningham. "Dog killed by Yowie" (Darwin, Australia: NT News, April 2, 2009).

42. Nick Redfern. *The Bigfoot Book: The Encyclopedia of Sasquatch, Yeti and Cryptid Primates* (Canton, MI: Visible Ink Press, 2016).

43. Tony Healy and Paul Cropper. *The Yowie: In Search of Australia's Bigfoot* (Sydney, Australia: Strange Nation, 2006).

44. Darren Naish. "What to make of the Yowie?" (Tetrapod Zoology (blog), 2010).

45. Micaela Hambrett. "Amid Sightings and Claims of a Cover-up, Could the Lithgow Panther Actually Exist?" *ABC News* (ABC News, June 14, 2018), https://www.abc.net.au/news/2018-06-13/could-the-lithgow-panther-actually-exist/9116232.

46. Kietley Isrin. "Hawkesbury Panther or Big Cat Alpaca Attack?" *Hawkesbury Gazette* (Fairfax Media, November 9, 2011). http://www.hawkesburygazette.com.au/news/local/news/general/hawkesbury-panther-or-big-cat-alpaca-attack/2352352.aspx.

47. "Hunt for the Black Panther." *The Sydney Morning Herald* (Nine Entertainment, February 27, 2005). https://www.smh.com.au/national/hunt-for-the-black-panther-20050227-gdkti5.html.

48. Phoebe Loomes. "Big Cats Sightings: Black Panther Caught on Video in Sydney's North Shore." *news.com.au* (Nationwide News Pty Ltd, July 23, 2020). https://www.news.com.au/technology/science/animals/big-cats-sightings-black-panther-caught-on-video-in-sydneys-north-shore/news-story/0d046d80d3b0e764c21a287a3ef061b9.

49. Phoebe Loomes. "Secretive Instagram Stars 'Convinced' They've Found Evidence of Big Cats in Blue Mountains." *news.com.au* (Nationwide News Pty Ltd, April 26, 2021). https://www.news.com.au/technology/science/animals/secretive-instagram-stars-convinced-theyve-found-evidence-of-big-cats-in-blue-mountains/news-story/d7f568765ee953c7727df51c892bef21.

50. See Note 49.

51. See Note 51.

52. See Note 49.

53. See Note 49.

54. See Note 49.

2. CHINA

1. Oliver D. Smith. *The Wildman of China: The Search for the Yeren* (Sino-Platonic Papers, 2021). https://hcommons.org/deposits/item/hc:35129.
2. See Note 59.
3. Sigrid Schmalzer. "'From Legend to Science,' and Back Again? Bigfoot, Science, and the People in Post-Máo China" in *The People's Peking Man: Popular Science and Human Identity in Twentieth-Century China* (Chicago, IL: University of Chicago Press, 2008): 429–497.
4. See Note 61.
5. Zhou Guoxing. "Fifty Years of Tracking the Chinese Wildman." *The Relict Hominoid Inquiry* 1 (2012): 118-141.
6. See Note 59.
7. See Note 61.
8. See Note 61.
9. "Search for Ape Man Continues against the Odds." *China.org.cn* (China Daily, October 12, 2010). http://www.china.org.cn/china/2010-10/12/content_21102561.htm.
10. See Note 67.
11. See Note 63.
12. See Note 61.
13. See Note 61.
14. Benjamin Haas. "'Dream Come True' for Moon as Korean Leaders Make Mountain Pilgrimage." *The Guardian* (Guardian News and Media, September 20, 2018). https://www.theguardian.com/world/2018/sep/20/dream-come-true-moon-jae-in-korean-leaders-mountain-pilgrimage.
15. Reuters. "China's 'Loch Ness Monster' Resurfaces." *The Sydney Morning Herald* (Nine Entertainment, July 16, 2003). https://www.smh.com.au/national/chinas-loch-ness-monster-resurfaces-20030716-gdh3s5.html.
16. Associated Press. "Chinese Swear Gold Monster Inhabits Lake." *Wilmington Morning Star* (August 8, 1986).
17. See Note 73.

18. "Chinese Nessie 'Alive and Well.'" *CNN.com* (Time Warner, July 31, 2002). http://edition.cnn.com/2002/WORLD/asiapcf/east/07/31/china.monster/.

19. See Note 73.

20. He Na. "'Monster' of Tianchi Lake sighted." *chinadaily.com.cn* (China Daily, July 11, 2007). http://www.chinadaily.com.cn/english/doc/2005-07/11/content_458959.htm.

21. "'Tianchi Monster' Caught on Film." People's Daily Online (September 10, 2007). http://en.people.cn/90001/90781/90879/6258937.html.

22. Luke Hawker. "China's Loch Ness Monster SPOTTED? Photographer Captures Bizarre Image at Mysterious Lake." *Express.co.uk* (Express Newspapers, October 22, 2020). https://www.express.co.uk/news/world/1350929/china-news-sea-creature-loch-ness-monster-Lake-Tianchi-pictures-video.

23. See Note 76.

24. *Blue Tiger* was reprinted by Coachwhip Publications in 2007.

25. Roy C. Andrews, *Camps and Trails in China* (New York City, New York: D. Appleton and Company, 1918).

26. J. Goodrich, Lynam, A., Miquelle, D., Wibisono, H., Kawanishi, K., Pattanavibool, A., Htun, S., Tempa, T., Karki, J., Jhala, Y. & Karanth, U. *Panthera tigris. The IUCN Red List of Threatened Species* (2015). https://dx.doi.org/10.2305/IUCN.UK.2015-2.RLTS.T15955A50659951.en.

27. Karl Shuker. *Mystery Cats of the World Revisited: Blue Tigers, King Cheetahs, Black Cougars, Spotted Lions, and More* (Charlottesville, Virginia: Anomalist Books, 2020).

28. "Amur Tiger Ecology." Wildlife Conservation Society. https://russia.wcs.org/en-us/Wildlife/Amur-Tigers/Amur-Tiger-Ecology.aspx.

29. Esther Inglis-Arkell. "Could the mythical blue tiger actually exist?" *Gizmodo* (G/O Media Inc., September 19, 2013). https://gizmodo.com/could-the-mythical-blue-tiger-actually-exist-1331164937.

3. INDIA

1. Luke Harding. "'Monkey man' causes panic across Delhi." *The Guardian* (Guardian News & Media Limited, May 17, 2001), https://www.theguardian.com/world/2001/may/18/lukeharding.

2. S K Verma & D K Srivastava. "A Study on mass Hysteria (Monkey Men?) Victims in East Delhi." *Indian Journal of Medical Sciences* 57, no. 8 (2003): 355-360

3. Benjamin Radford. "The Monkey Man Panic: 20 Years Later." *Skeptical Inquirer* (Center for Inquiry, Inc., May 21, 2021). https://skepticalinquirer.org/exclusive/the-monkey-man-panic-20-years-later/.

4. See Note 90.

5. The May reports happened during a heat wave and rolling blackouts.

6. See Note 89.

7. See Note 90.

8. A. R. Radcliffe-Brown. *The Andaman Islanders* (Cambridge, England: Cambridge University Press, 1922).

9. Aparna Unni. "Of Myths and Legends: The 'Kallana' Story." *The New Indian Express* (February 13, 2013). https://www.newindianexpress.com/cities/kochi/2013/feb/13/of-myths-and-legends-the-kallana-story-450103.html.

10. See Note 96.

11. See Note 96.

12. "Bornean Elephant." World Wildlife Fund (World Wildlife Fund Inc., n.d.). https://www.worldwildlife.org/species/bornean-elephant.

13. Alastair Lawson. "On the trail of the 'Indian yeti.'" *BBC News* (BBC, June 17, 2008). http://news.bbc.co.uk/1/hi/world/south_asia/7457894.stm.

14. See Note 100.

15. Richard Freeman. *Adventures in Cryptozoology: Hunting for Yetis, Mongolian Deathworms and Other Not-So-Mythical Monsters* (Coral Gables, Florida: Mango Publishing, 2019).

16. See Note 100.

17. Alastair Lawson. "'Yeti hair' to get DNA analysis." *BBC News* (BBC, July 25, 2008). http://news.bbc.co.uk/2/hi/south_asia/7525060.stm.
18. See Note 104.

4. INDONESIA

1. Debbie Martyr. "The Other Orang" (BBC Wildlife, 1993).
2. Bernard Heuvelmans. *On The Track of Unknown Animals* (Cambridge, MA: MIT Press, 1972).
3. Nick Redfern. *The Bigfoot Book: The Encyclopedia of Sasquatch, Yeti and Cryptid Primates* (Canton, MI: Visible Ink Press, 2016).
4. Richard Roberts. "Villagers speak of the small, hairy Ebu Gogo." *The Daily Telegraph* (October 2008, 2004). https://www.primates.com/ebu-gogo/index.html.
5. Richard Freeman. "On the trail of the orang pendek, Sumatra's mystery ape." *The Guardian* (Guardian News and Media, September 8, 2011). https://www.theguardian.com/science/blog/2011/sep/08/orang-pendek-sumatra-mystery-ape.
6. Cara Biega. "Ape-Man" from *Is It Real?* (TV episode) (National Geographic, Washington, DC, 2006).
7. See Note 106.
8. Karl Shuker. *The Beasts That Hide from Man* (New York, NY: Paraview Press, 2003).
9. Quentin Phillipps and Karen Phillipps. *Phillipps' Field Guide to the Mammals of Borneo and Their Ecology: Sabah, Sarawak, Brunei, and Kalimantan* (Princeton, New Jersey: Princeton University Press, 2016).
10. See Note 113.
11. Jonathan Maberry and David F. Kramer. *The Cryptopedia* (New York, NY: Kensington Publishing Corp., 2007).
12. Ken Gerhard. *Encounters With Flying Humanoids* (Woodbury, MN: Llewellyn Publications, 2013).
13. Michael Newton. *Hidden Animals: A Field Guide to Batsquatch, Chupacabra, and Other Elusive Creatures* (Santa Barbara, CA: Greenwood Press, 2009).

14. Ivan T. Sanderson and Ernest Bartels. "The One True Batman." *Fate Magazine* 19, 1966).

15. Deena West Budd. *The Weiser Field Guide to Cryptozoology* (San Francisco, CA: Weiser Books, 2010).

16. Jonathan Maberry and David F. Kramer. *The Cryptopedia* (New York, NY: Kensington Publishing Corp., 2007).

17. Robert. Benjamin. *Unknown Creatures* (Morrisville, NC: Lulu Press, 2009).

18. Karl Shuker. *The Beasts That Hide From Man* (New York, NY: Paraview Publishing, 2003).

19. Charles Miller. *Cannibal Caravan* (New York, NY: Lee Furman, 1939).

20. P. Jackson and E. Kemf. *Wanted alive! Tigers in the wild: 1994 WWF species status report* (World Wildlife Fund, 1994).

21. J. Seidensticker. "Bearing witness: observations on the extinction of *Panthera tigris balica* and *Panthera tigris sondaica*" in *Tigers of the world: the biology, biopolitics, management, and conservation of an endangered species* (Park Ridge, NJ: Noyes Publications, 1987).

22. Greg Breining. "What's Our Zoo Got to Do With It?" (Minnesota Conservation Volunteer, Apple Valley, 2002).

23. Parwito. "Woman Climber Killed on Mount Merbabu, Suspected by Tiger" (translated from Indonesian) (Detik News, Magelang, 2008).

24. "Tiger rumours swirl below Indon volcano" (*The Sydney Morning Herald*, 2010).

25. PROFAUNA. "Sight of Javan Tiger in Mt. Arjuno Went Viral" (Indonesia, 2018).

26. See Note 130.

27. PROFAUNA. Personal correspondence with author (2018).

28. Jon Emont. "Tiger Species Thought Extinct Is Possibly Spotted in Indonesia" (*The New York Times*, 2017).

5. JAPAN

1. "Akkorokamui." Yokai (n.d.). https://yokai.com/akkorokamui/.

2. Brent Swancer. "The Mystery Monster Octopus of Japan's Far North." Mysterious Universe (April 28, 2017). https://mysteri

ousuniverse.org/2017/04/the-mystery-monster-octopus-of-japans-far-north.

3. See Note 134.

4. See Note 135.

5. John Batchelor. *The Ainu and Their Folk-lore* (Religious Tract Society: 1901): 530.

6. See Note 135.

7. See Note 135.

8. Brad Steiger. *Real Monsters, Gruesome Critters, and Beasts from the Darkside* (Canton, MI: Visible Ink Press, 2010): 103.

9. See Note 141.

10. See Note 141.

11. I could not find reference to the reported colour of the hibagon in the sources consulted for this chapter, minus an uncited source on a blog saying that its fur was black. The town of Shobara has a statue and a hibagon mascot, both with red fur.

12. Kohei Higashitani, "Japan's 'Bigfoot' still influences Hiroshima town after 50 years," *The Asahi Shimbun* (August 13, 2020), https://www.asahi.com/ajw/articles/13584940.

13. See Note 145.

14. . See Note 145.

15. See Note 145.

16. Janet & Colin Bord, *Alien Animals* (London, England: Granada Publishing, 1980).

17. Interestingly, the honorific "-kun" is typically masculine, which contradicts the mythology of the Issie.

18. "Do you know that Issie, the Japanese Loch Ness monster, lives in Ikeda Lake?" *Peak Experience Japan* (Eurex Co., Ltd., 19 August 2019). https://www.peak-experience-japan.com/blog/505.

19. Jessica Kozuka. "Meet Issie, Japan's very own Loch Ness Monster." *SoraNews24* (Socio Corporation, September 30, 2014). https://soranews24.com/2014/09/30/meet-issie-japans-very-own-loch-ness-monster/.

20. Malcolm Robinson. *The Monsters of Loch Ness (The History and the Mystery)* [2016]: 42.

21. George M. Eberhart. *Mysterious Creatures: A Guide to Cryptozoology* (Santa Barbara, CA: ABC-CLIO, 2002): 251.

22. "Lake Ikeda." *GaijinPotTravel* (GPlusMedia Inc., n.d.). https://travel.gaijinpot.com/lake-ikeda/.

23. See Note 153.

24. George M. Eberhart. *Mysterious Creatures: A Guide to Cryptozoology* (Santa Barbara, CA: ABC-CLIO, 2002).

25. See Note 158.

26. See Note 158.

27. "Japan's Own Sea Serpent." *NewsWeek* (NewsWeek Digital LLC, August 10, 1987). https://www.newsweek.com/japans-own-sea-serpent-172406.

28. Kenzo Moriguchi. "Town touting mythical snake find; is 'rare' creature really a cash cow?" *Japan Times* (June 16, 2001). https://www.japantimes.co.jp/news/2001/06/16/national/town-touting-mythical-snake-find-is-rare-creature-really-a-cash-cow.

29. Craig Boutland. *Gashadokuro the Giant Skeleton and Other Legendary Creatures of Japan* (Milwaukee, Wisconsin: Gareth Stevens Inc., 2018): 26-27.

30. Brent Swancer. "Tsuchinoko, Part Two." *CryptoZooNews* (Loren Coleman, November 2, 2008). http://www.cryptozoonews.com/tsuchinoko-3/.

31. See Note 164.

32. See Note 164.

6. MALAYSIA

1. N.W. Kit. *The Persistent Dead: Antiquarian Ghosts and Other Stories* (Singapore: Partridge Singapore, 2015).

2. Jonathan Kent. "Hunting for Malaysia's 'Bigfoot'" (BBC online, 2006).

3. Loren Coleman. "Vincent Chow and the Photographs" (Cryptomundo, 2006).

4. Nicholas Cheng. "Giant footprints are not that of Bigfoot, says Wildlife Department" (The Star Online, Petaling, Jaya, 2013).

5. Gregory Forth. *Images of the Wildman in Southeast Asia: An Anthropological Perspective* (New York, NY: Routledge, 2008).

6. George M. Eberhart. *Mysterious Creatures: A Guide to Cryptozoology* (Santa Barbara, CA: ABC-CLIO, 2002).

7. Michael Newton. *Encyclopedia of Cryptozoology: A Global Guide to Hidden Animals and Their Pursuers* (Jefferson, NC: McFarland & Company, 2005).

8. Sarah Hartwell. "Anomalous Felids" (Messybeast, United Kingdom, accessed 27 April 2017).

9. Karl Shuker. *The Beasts That Hide from Man* (New York, NY: Paraview Press, 2003).

10. George M. Eberhart. *Mysterious Creatures: A Guide to Cryptozoology* (Santa Barbara, CA: ABC-CLIO, 2002).

11. Richard Freeman. "Beyond the Lake of Seven Peaks: The Search for Sumatra's Mystery Beasts" (Centre for Fortean Zoology, Bideford, accessed 27 April 2017).

7. MONGOLIA

1. Nathan Wenzel. "The Legend of the Almas: A Comparative and Critical Analysis." *Independent Study Project (ISP) Collection* (209). https://digitalcollections.sit.edu/isp_collection/801.

2. See Note 178.

3. See Note 178.

4. See Note 178.

5. Nikolai Przhevalskii. *Mongolia, the Tangut Country, and the Solitudes of Northern Tibet, Being a Narrative of Three Years' Travel in Eastern High Asia* (S. Low, Marston, Searle, & Rivington, 1876).

6. See Note 178.

7. Arthur Ochs "Punch" Sulzberger, ed. "Soviet Scientist Believes 'Snowmen' Are Neanderthal Survivors." *The New York Times* (February 18, 1964). https://www.nytimes.com/1964/02/18/archives/soviet-scientist-believes-snowmen-are-neanderthal-survivors.html.

8. Daniel Harris. "The Mongolian death worm." Unexplained Mysteries (June 26, 2007). https://www.unexplained-mysteries.com/column.php?id=98249.

9. Adam Davies. "Death Worms!" Fortean Times (April 2004). Archived at https://web.archive.org/web/20121126032712/http://www.forteantimes.com/features/articles/158/death_worm.html.

10. Josh Gates. *Destination Truth* (New York, NY: Simon and Schuster, 2011): 89.

11. Karl Shuker. *The Unexplained: An Illustrated Guide to the World's Natural and Paranormal Mysteries* (East Bridgewater, MA: JG Press, 1996).

12. See Note 187.

13. Roy Chapman Andrews. *On The Trail Of Ancient Man* (London, England: G. P. Putnam's Son, 1926).

14. "The 'Mongolian Death Worm', fact or fantasy?" *The Observers* (France24, June 10, 2010). https://observers.france24.com/en/20090810-mongolian-death-worm-fact-or-fantasy.

15. Benjamin Radford. "Mongolian Death Worm: Elusive Legend of the Gobi Desert." *LiveScience* (Future US, Inc., June 21, 2014).

8. NEPAL

1. *The Abominable Snowman* (1957). Hammer Films (Exclusive Media Group, 2011). Archived at https://web.archive.org/web/20111227211934/http://www.hammerfilms.com/productions/film/filmid/310/the-abominable-snowman.

2. Joe Smith. "The Yeti: A Story of Scientific Misunderstanding." *Cool Green Science* (The Nature Conservancy, April 2, 2018). https://blog.nature.org/science/2018/04/02/the-yeti-a-story-of-scientific-misunderstanding/.

3. Laurence Waddell. *Among the Himalayas* (Westminster, England: Archibald Constable And Co., 1899).

4. Matthew Hill. "Tracing the origins of a 'yeti's finger'." *BBC News* (British Broadcasting Corp., December 27, 2011). https://www.bbc.com/news/science-environment-16264752.

5. Michael Gill. *Edmund Hillary: A Biography* (Nelson, NZ: Potton & Burton, 2017).

6. Marca Burns. "Report on a Sample of Skin and Hair from the Khumjung Yeti Scalp." *Genus* 18, no. 1: 80–88. JSTOR 29787501.

7. Charles Haviland. "'Yeti prints' found near Everest." *BBC News* (British Broadcasting Corp., December 1, 2007). http://news.bbc.co.uk/1/hi/world/south_asia/7122705.stm.

8. Benjamin Radford. "The Yeti: Asia's Abominable Snowman." *Live Science* (Future US Inc., November 27, 2017).

9. NEW ZEALAND

1. Nick Redfern. *The Bigfoot Book: The Encyclopedia of Sasquatch, Yeti and Cryptid Primates* (Canton, MI: Visible Ink Press, 2016).
2. Peter Turner. *National Geographic Traveler: New Zealand* (Washington, DC: National Geographic, 2009).
3. Robyn Jenkin. *New Zealand Mysteries* (Auckland, NZ: The Bush Press of New Zealand, 1996).
4. James Cook. *A Voyage Towards the South Pole and Round the World, Volume 1* (Bibliolife DBA of Bibilio Bazaar II LLC, 2015).
5. T. M. Hocken. *Contributions to the Early History of New Zealand.* (London, England: Sampson Low, Marston And Company, 1898).
6. J. S. Watson. "The New Zealand 'otter'" (Records of the Canterbury Museum 7. 1960).
7. John Tasker. *Quest Aotearoa – Volume One* (Morrisville, NC: Lulu Enterprises, 2012).
8. G. A. Pollock. "The South Island otter – an addendum" (Proceedings of the New Zealand Ecological Society 21, 1974).
9. See Note 206.
10. Bernard Heuvelmans. *On The Track of Unknown Animals* (Cambridge, MA: MIT Press, 1972).
11. Francis Darwin, ed. *The life and letters of Charles Darwin, including an autobiographical chapter* (London, England: John Murray, 1887).
12. Bernard Heuvelmans. *Natural History of Hidden Animals* (New York, NY: Routledge, 2010).
13. R. C. Bruce. "On A Maori Waiata" (Presentation at the Wellington Philosophical Society, October 1892).
14. See Note 213.
15. C. M. Miskelly. "The Identity of the Hakawai" (*Notornis and Birds New Zealand* 34, Wellington, 1987).
16. Robyn Jenkin. *New Zealand Mysteries* (Auckland, NZ: The Bush Press of New Zealand, 1996).
17. A. H. McLintock, ed. "Animals, Mythical," from *An Encyclopaedia of New Zealand* (Wellington, NZ: 1966).
18. See Note 217.
19. "The Kumi" (*Wanganui Herald*, 1898).

20. Geoffrey R. Clark, Peter Petchey, Matthew S. McGlone, and Peter Bristow. "Faunal and floral remains from Earnscleugh Cave, Central Otago, New Zealand" (*Journal of the Royal Society of New Zealand* 26, no. 3, Wellington, 1996).

21. F. W. Hutton. "On a supposed rib of the kumi, or ngarara" (Transactions and proceedings of the New Zealand Institute 31, 1899).

22. Tony Whittaker. "Kawekaweau – Myth Or Monster?" (New Zealand Geographic).

23. Aaron M. Bauer and Anthony P. Russell. "*Hoplodactylus Delcourti* (Reptilia: Gekkonidae) and the Kawekaweau Of Maori Folklore" (*Journal of Ethnobiology*, 1987).

24. See Note 222.

25. Michael Szabo. "Huia, The Sacred Bird" (New Zealand Geographic).

26. Michael Szabo. "Huia" in C. M. Miskelly (ed.) (*New Zealand Birds Online*, 2013).

27. W. L. Buller. *A history of the birds of New Zealand* (London, England: Van Vorst, 1888).

28. See Note 227.

29. See Note 225.

30. Caroline Wood. "Hunting the last huia" (Forest & Bird (blog), 2017).

31. See Note 230.

32. Jack Fletcher. "Huia-like bird could sing from the branches once again, but what are the limits?" (*Stuff New Zealand*, 2017).

33. B. Michaux. "Laughing owl" (*New Zealand Birds Online*, 2017)

34. Deane Lewis. "Laughing Owl – *Sceloglaux albifacies*" (The Owl Pages, 2013).

35. "Whekau, the laughing owl" (*New Zealand Birds Online*, 2019)

36. R. St. Paul, and H. R. McKenzie. "A bushman's seventeen years of noting birds, Part F (Conclusion of series) – Notes on other native birds" (*Notornis and Birds New Zealand* 24, issue 2, Wellington, 1977).

37. A. Blackburn. "A 1927 record of the Laughing Owl" (*Notornis and Birds New Zealand* 29, issue 1, Wellington, 1982).

38. Brian Parkinson. *The Travelling Naturalist Around New Zealand* (London, England: Century Hutchinson, 1989).

39. John Hall-Jones. "Rare Fiordland birds" (*Notornis and New Zealand Birds* 8, issue 7, Wellington, 1960).

40. G. R. Williams and M. Harrison. "The Laughing Owl *Sceloglaux albifacies* (Gray. 1844): A general survey of a near-extinct species" (*Notornis and New Zealand Birds* 19, issue 1, Wellington, 1972).

41. Errol Fuller. *Extinct Birds* (2nd ed.) (Oxford, England: Oxford University Press, 2000).

42. "New Zealand Greater Short-tailed Bat" (*EDGE of Existence*, London).

43. Simon Nathan. "Greater short-tailed bat (3rd of 4)" (*Te Ara: the Encyclopedia of New Zealand*, Wellington, 2015).

44. C. F. J. O'Donnell. "New Zealand Greater Short-tailed Bat (*Mystacina robusta*)" (*The IUCN Red List of Threatened Species*, Cambridge, 2008).

45. C. F. J. O'Donnell, K. M. Borkin, J. E. Christie, B. Lloyd, S. Parsons, and R. A. Hitchmough. "Conservation status of New Zealand bats, 2017" (New Zealand Department of Conservation, Wellington, 2018).

46. Bernard Heuvelmans. *On The Track of Unknown Animals* (Cambridge, MA: MIT Press, 1972).

47. George Perry, Andrew B. Wheeler, Jamie R. Wood, and Janet M. Wilmshurst: "A high-precision chronology for the rapid extinction of New Zealand moa (*Aves, Dinornithiformes*)" (*Quaternary Science Reviews* 105, 2014).

48. Charles Gould. *Mythical Monsters* (London, England: W.H. Allen & Co., 1886).

49. Atholl Anderson. "On Evidence For The Survival Of Moa In European Fiordland" (*New Zealand Journal of Ecology* 12, Dunedin, 1989).

50. Trevor H. Worthy. "Moa – Moa and people" (*Te Ara: the Encyclopedia of New Zealand*, Wellington, 2015).

51. Annie Potts, Philip Armstrong, and Deidre Brown. *A New Zealand Book of Beasts* (Auckland, NZ: Auckland University Press, 2013).

52. Bruce Spittle, *Moa Sightings, Volume 1* (Dunedin, NZ: Paua Press Limited, 2010).

53. Mike Searle. "Moa" from *Animal X* (TV episode) (Storyteller Media Group, Perth, 2002).

10. PAPUA NEW GUINEA

1. Errol Fuller. *Lost Animals: Extinction and the Photographic Record* (London, England: Bloomsbury Publishing, 2013).

2. Karl Shuker. "The New Guinea Thylacine – Crying Wolf in Irian Jaya?" ShukerNature (blog), 2013).

3. George M. Eberhart. *Mysterious Creatures: A Guide to Cryptozoology* (Santa Barbara, CA: ABC-CLIO, 2002).

4. Jamie Hall. "Thylacine and Queensland Tiger" (*The Cryptid Zoo* (blog), 2005).

5. Corrina Carter. "The Thylacine: A Striped Haunting" (*Kenyon Review* online, Gambier, 2016).

6. Helen Pilcher. *Bring Back the King: The New Science of De-extinction* (London, England: Bloomsbury Publishing, 2016).

7. Alfred O. Walker. "The Rhinoceros in New Guinea" (*Nature* 11, no. 274, London 1875).

8. A. B. Meyer. "The Rhinoceros in New Guinea" (*Nature* 11, no. 275, London, 1875).

9. Karl Shuker. *The Beasts That Hide from Man* (New York, NY: Paraview Press, 2003).

10. Karl Shuker. "Dung-heaps, Devil-Pigs, and Monckton's Gazeka" (ShukerNature (blog), 2014).

11. See Note 163.

12. See Note 162.

13. See Note 162.

14. Jonathan Maberry and David F. Kramer. *The Cryptopedia* (New York, NY: Kensington Publishing Corp., 2007).

15. Nick Redfern. *The Monster Book: Creatures, Beasts and Fiends of Nature* (Detroit, MI: Visible Ink Press, 2017).

16. Ishaan Tharoor. "Ropen" (*TIME Magazine*, New York City, 2009).

17. Darren Naish. *Hunting Monsters: Cryptozoology and the Reality Behind the Myths* (London, England: Arcturus Publishing Limited, 2017).

18. See Note 269.

19. See Note 269.

20. Glen J. Kuban. "Living Pterosaurs ('pterodactyls')?" (Glen Kuban (blog), 2016).

11. PHILIPPINES

1. Gilbert Bayoran. "Creature terrorizing residents of farms" (*The Visayan Daily Star*, Bacolod City, 13 June 2008).

2. Erwin Ambo Delilan. "Residents on alert vs 'wild monkey'" (*Sun Star*, Cebu City, 16 June 2008).

3. Nick Redfern. *The Bigfoot Book: The Encyclopedia of Sasquatch, Yeti and Cryptid Primates* (Canton, MI: Visible Ink Press, 2016).

4. Damiana Eugenio. *Philippine Folk Literature: An Anthology* (Quezon City, Philippines: University of the Philippines Press, 1982).

5. Erwin Ambo Delilan. "'Amomongo' frightens villagers in Negros." (ABS-CBN News, Quezon City, 2008).

6. John U. Wolff. *A dictionary of Cebuano Visayan, Volume I* (Ithaca, NY: Cornell University Library, 1972).

7. Jordan Clark. "Kapre, The Tree Dweller" (Creatures Of Philippine Mythology, 2015).

8. Bernard Heuvelmans., *On The Track of Unknown Animals* (Cambridge, MA: MIT Press, 1972).

9. See Note 279.

10. Theresa Bane. *Encyclopedia of Beasts and Monsters in Myth, Legend and Folklore* (Jefferson, NC: McFarland & Company, Inc., 2016).

11. Richard Warren Lieban. *Cebuano Sorcery; Malign Magic in the Philippines* (Berkeley, CA: University of California Press, 1967).

12. Jamie Farter *Listverse.com's Ultimate Book of Bizarre Lists* (Berkeley, CA: Ulysses Press, 2010).

13. Jennifer Rivkin. *Searching for El Chupacabra* (New York, NY: PowerKids Press, 2015).

14. See Note 286.

12. RUSSIA

1. George M. Eberhart. *Mysterious Creatures: A Guide to Cryptozoology* (Santa Barbara, California: ABC-CLIO, 2002).

2. Stan Gooch. *The Dream Culture of the Neanderthals: Guardians of the Ancient Wisdom* (Rochester, VT: Inner Traditions, 2006).

3. See Note 288.

4. Ashot Margaryan, Mikkel-Holger S. Sinding, Christian Carøe, Vladimir Yamshchikov, Igor Burtsev, and M. Thomas P. Gilbert. "The genomic origin of Zana of Abkhazia." *Advanced Genetics* 2, no. 2 (2021). https://doi.org/10.1002/ggn2.10051.

5. Erin McCann. "What Is The Brosno Dragon And Has It Really Been Lurking In A Russian Lake Since The 13th Century?" *Graveyard Shift* (Ranker, July 2, 2021), https://www.ranker.com/list/brosno-dragon-russian-cryptid/erin-mccann.

6. Wade Wainio. "The Brosno dragon of western Russia!" *1428Elm* (blog) (Fansided, July 3, 2019). https://1428elm.com/2019/07/03/call-of-the-cryptid-brosno-dragon-russia/.

7. See Note 293.

8. Rob Murphy. "Brosno Dragon," Cryptopia (January 6, 2010). https://www.cryptopia.us/site/2010/01/brosno-dragon-russia/.

13. SINGAPORE

1. Nick Redfern. *The Bigfoot Book: The Encyclopedia of Sasquatch, Yeti and Cryptid Primates* (Canton, MI: Visible Ink Press, 2015).

2. See Note 296.

3. Chris Ashton. "Searching for 'Singapore's Bigfoot': Step inside the city's mysterious forest." *YourSingapore* (2017). https://travel.nine.com.au/destinations/bukit-timah-singapore-monkey-man-sighting-and-tours/8ff5b26e-edb5-4e6c-af1f-320a562ac706.

4. Tanya Ong. "Some people in S'pore believe they've seen the Bukit Timah Monkey Man." *Mothership* (February 9, 2018). https://mothership.sg/2018/02/bukit-timah-monkey-man/.

5. See Note 299.

14. SRI LANKA

1. A. T. Rambukwella and S. J. Kadirgamar. "The Nittaewo – The Legendary Pygmies of Ceylon." *The Journal of the Ceylon Branch of the Royal Asiatic Society of Great Britain & Ireland New Series* 8, No. 2 (1963): 265-290. https://www.jstor.org/stable/45377766.

2. See Note 301.

3. Bernard Heuvelmans. *On The Track of Unknown Animals* (Cambridge, MA: MIT Press, 1972).

4. See Note 303.

5. Hugh Neville quoted in *Nittaewo, The Hobbits of Sri Lanka: An Analysis of the Legend* by Pradeep A. Jayatunga: 24 and 73.

6. Ven. Thambugala Anandasiri quoted in *Nittaewo, The Hobbits of Sri Lanka: An Analysis of the Legend* by Pradeep A. Jayatunga: 28

7. Frederick Lewis. "Notes on an Exploration in Eastern Uya, and Southern Panama Patch." *The Journal of the Ceylon Branch of the Royal Asiatic Society of Great Britain & Ireland* 23, no. 67 (1914): 276-293.

8. Andy McGrath. *Beasts of the World: Hairy Humanoids* (Minneapolis, MN: Hanger 1 Publishing, 2022).

9. See Note 308.

10. See Note 305.

11. Pradeep A. Jayatunga, *Nittaewo, The Hobbits of Sri Lanka: An Analysis of the Legend* (Battaramulla, Sri Lanka: Neptune Publications, 2010): 74–75.

12. Personal communications with Pradeep A. Jayatunga, March 2, 2022, via Zoom.

13. "Ceylon's Devil Bird." *The Sunday Times* no. 18, September 15, 1906. Archived at https://trove.nla.gov.au/newspaper/article/126269451.

14. "Devil Bird of Ceylon." *Taranaki Herald*, Volume LIV, Issue 13444, 11 April 1907, page 2. Archived at https://paperspast.natlib.govt.nz/newspapers/TH19070411.2.7.

15. Ria Rameez. "Seven Mythical Creatures That Supposedly Haunt Sri Lanka." Roar Media (June 6, 2016). https://roar.media/english/life/srilanka-life/local-demons-ghosts-crazy-myths.

16. See Note 313.

17. See Note 315.

15. TURKEY

1. Lauren Tousignant. "Divers looking for Lake Van Monster uncover this secret instead." *New York Post* (NYP Holdings, Inc., November 21, 2017). https://nypost.com/2017/11/21/divers-looking-for-lake-van-monster-uncover-this-secret-instead/.

2. See Note 318.

3. "Sea monster or monster hoax?," *CNN* (June 12, 1997). Archived at https://web.archive.org/web/20220411161408/http://www.cnn.com/WORLD/9706/12/fringe/turkey.monster/.

4. See Note 320.

5. Sean Sheehan and Jui Lin Yong. *Turkey* (New York, NY: Cavendish Square, 2014): 53.

6. Nathan Robert Brown. *The Complete Idiot's Guide to the Paranormal* (London, UK: DK Publishing, 2010).

7. See Note 320.

16. VIETNAM

1. Stanely Karnow. *Vietnam: A history* (New York, NY: Penguin Books, 1997).

2. John MacKinnon. *In Search of the Red Ape* (New York, NY: Holt, Rinehart and Winston, 1974): 113.

3. Michael Newton. *The Encyclopedia of Cryptozoology: A Global Guide to Hidden Animals and Their Pursuers* (Jefferson, NC: McFarland & Company, 2005).

4. Nick Redfern. *The Bigfoot Book: The Encyclopedia of Sasquatch, Yeti and Cryptid Primates* (Canton, MI: Visible Ink Press, 2015).

5. Vern Weitzel. "Nguoi Rung, Vietnamese Forest People, Wildman: mythical or missing ape" (Australia Vietnam Science Technology Link, Belconnen, 1998).

6. Vern Weitzel. "The Nguoi Rung Footprint: the rather fuzzy evidence is finally published" (Australia Vietnam Science Technology Link, Belconnen, 1996).

7. See Note 327.

8. Loren Coleman and Patrick Huyghe. *The Field Guide to Bigfoot and Other Mystery Primates* (New York, NY: Anomalist Books, 2006).

9. Karl Shuker. *The New Zoo: New and Rediscovered Animals of the Twentieth Century* (Cornwall, England: Stratus Books Limited, 2002).

10. See Note 333.

11. Damien Larkins and Dan Prosser. "Cow caught chewing on a large python in outback northern Australia." *ABC News Australia* (October 28, 2020). https://www.abc.net.au/news/2020-10-28/cow-eating-snake-photos-outback-australia/12822382.

12. Eric J. Bartelink, Krista E. Latham, Michael Finnegan, eds. *New Perspectives in Forensic Human Skeletal Identification* (Amsterdam, Netherlands: Elsevier, 2017): 146.

Carol Scott developed an interest in cryptozoology after catching a late-night episode of *Animal X*. This interest and her previous work in journalism, led her to research and write her first book, *The Cryptids of Asia and Oceania: The Myths and Historical Roots of Undiscovered Creatures.*

She currently works in marketing and lives with her two cats, Wallace and Asparagus in Ontario, Canada.